semifirm goat cheese

mixed milk cheese

goat blues

hard goat cheese

hembert

ricotta salata

feta

aged cheddar

buches

semifirm goat cheese

aged jack

aged gouda

manchego

goatcheese

goatcheese

Maggie Foard

Anderson, S.C.

AND

Gibbs Smith, Publisher
TO ENRICH AND INSPIRE HUMANKIND
Salt Lake City | Charleston | Santa Fe | Santa Barbara

First Edition
12 11 10 09 08   5 4 3 2 1

Published by
Gibbs Smith
P.O. Box 667
Layton, Utah 84041

1-800.835.4993 orders
www.gibbs-smith.com

Designed and produced by Debra McQuiston
Printed and bound in Hong Kong

Library of Congress Cataloging-in-Publication Data

Foard, Maggie.
  Goat cheese / Maggie Foard.
     p. cm.
  ISBN-13: 978-1-4236-0368-9
  ISBN-10: 1-4236-0368-0
  1. Cookery (Goat cheese) 2. Goat cheese. I. Title.
  TX759.5.C48F63 2008
  641.6'73—dc22
                      2008004563

For Eric, the very heart of my kitchen

CONTENTS

acknowledgments

The idea of an entire cookbook devoted to goat cheese started as a laugh at a party with my friends, but once that little seed took hold in my brain, the idea began to grow on me. I have always loved to cook. All my life, I have expressed my creativity in the kitchen. Feeding people is somehow the thing I was born to do. The best part of life is cooking, eating, and sitting down together, fulfilling the desire to create something delicious for dinner just about every night. No day is complete for me without this ritual.

I have always had a secret desire to write a cookbook, and then along came goat cheese. As a recent discoverer of chèvre, a pure white goat's milk cheese, I had begun using it in daily food preparation, in place of other cheese and dairy. Everyone who walked through the door became a fresh victim for some creation I had just put together. At first, people kind of looked at me sideways. "Ugh—you mean this has goat cheese in it?" But it wasn't long before the telephone was ringing and they were asking me for the recipes. Suddenly, I had my own small army of recipe testers. And so began my own little goat cheese revolution.

I would like to thank the following people for all their help with this dream cookbook of mine: to my friend Gillian Allen for giving me that very first little shove in the right direction; to my friends for your willingness to taste and test all those experiments—thank you Molly Black, Nancy Whiting, Alma and Elena Scheer, Theresa Kpachavi, Lesa Horve and Finn Sukkestad, Amie Breed, Hilda Williams and Helena Pisani; and to my dear friend Sue Lagow for testing all those ricotta pancakes out on Josh's friends! To Jeanie Graham and Annabel Rorden for sharing the

recipe for Annabel's purse; to David Grisby for testing the brownie; to Karen Huck at Whole Foods, Redwood City, for answering a hundred questions and for the best cheese selection for miles around; to Cowgirl Creamery for stocking a wonderful coast-to-coast selection of new artisan goat cheeses as well as the best from Europe; to Bill Pagano for the really great advice; to Mark Toal for his great skill in portrait photography. Thanks to my publisher, Gibbs Smith, for taking a chance on me; to my editor, Katie Newbold, for her kind encouragement and sense of humor; to Debra McQuiston and the rest of the Gibbs Smith, Publisher staff for the beautiful layout; and to Karla Oliveira for believing in me and lighting the way.

Very special thanks to Lori Sang Hsu and Harlan Chapman, my photographers, for so many hours of hard work producing the photographs for this book; to Robyn Valarik and Stephania Serena for their beautiful styling and photo work; to Kathleen Downing for her friendship, help and real feedback on many of the recipes and for an endless stream of encouragement; to Dee Harley of Harley Farms Goat Dairy in Pescadero, California, for making the cheese that inspired me in the first place, for her interest in my project and for countless pounds of amazing goat cheese to experiment with. No wonder you were Farmer of the Year 2007!

Finally, I want to thank my husband, Jim, and my son, Eric, for building me the kitchen of my dreams and for being such good sports and eating whatever new mystery item was for dinner every night for almost two years.

introduction

There's a goat

Lesson 1: **One is never enough.**

It happened one morning in the midst of unpacking in my brand-new kitchen. The kitchen door burst open and in walked a goat! Since I'd never had a huge billy goat loose in my kitchen, I didn't know exactly what to do and stood dumbfounded. As he inspected the kitchen, I was surprised to see that his shoulders were as tall as my new center island, a full thirty-six-inches. The horns that had been disbudded as a kid were persistent and had grown back with a vengeance. Add in his head and neck, and that made him four-and-a-half-feet tall or more. Being barely five feet myself, this was more than a bit intimidating considering the horns were almost at eye level!

It was my goat, of course, and his name was Aladdin. It had only been a few days since my new kitchen addition was up and running. I was caught up in the excitement of unpacking all my sorely missed kitchen belongings, which had been packed away for the duration of the seemingly endless building project. I must have neglected to feed the barnyard that morning, and Aladdin, a large adolescent goat, simply wouldn't be ignored.

At first, I didn't know what to do, as a goat doesn't necessarily obey commands like a dog does. How will I get this goat back out to the barnyard? His recent growth spurt had necessitated the removal of his collar, which had grown snug on his neck, so I had no handle with which to lead him back out to the barnyard. No leash, no collar, no doggie obedience training to fall back on. Then it occurred to me: he was there to remind me that I'd forgotten

in my kitchen!

to feed him. So I just opened the kitchen door and headed out to the barnyard, picking up a flake of alfalfa grass on the way. He trailed just behind, rearing up now and then and jumping unusually high to celebrate his liberation from the pasture fence. I concentrated on not letting on that I feared the repercussions of those horns at my backside at any moment. How he had gotten out of the gate was not yet apparent. When he was happily back inside his paddock, munching away, I closed the gate thankfully and went back inside.

I was glad to see that Aladdin's appetite was back. This was the first time in weeks he'd been really interested in food. Our very old Nubian goat, Shannie, has passed away a few weeks previously. She had been Aladdin's adopted mother, and while she was skittish with people, she was very sure of herself with him. No matter how large he got, she saw herself as his boss, and he was her constant companion. When she died, we were all amazed at the amount of grief he displayed, and we had made a point to give him a little extra special attention.

Later that morning, I had a much bigger problem. He was back in the house and this time he wasn't hungry. Now what would I do? Left no other choice, I decided it was time to go play outside. I took the phone with me and dialed Harley Farms. "I think I need another goat."

goat's milk is superior to cow's

2 + 1= Cheese!

Many of the small goat dairies in the United States got started with just a couple of goats. The stories are all different, but the one thing that most of them have in common is that the goat owners hadn't actually planned on becoming cheese makers. What started as a hobby, a 4-H project or just a couple of dairy goats for a child allergic to milk turned into a small cheese-making operation and then a career. This recent phenomenon in the United States has produced a whole new age of talented and adventurous cheese makers. We suddenly have a huge and wonderful variety of artisan goat cheeses available all across the country.

There is nothing new about goat cheese. But with only a handful of goat dairies in this country just twenty years ago, most of the goat cheese you could buy had traveled across the Atlantic from Europe. In 2007, there were over 200 certified licensed goat dairies from coast to coast! Passionate farmer/cheese makers making everything from chèvre, feta, mozzarella and ricotta to Brie, cheddar, Goudas, blues, Parmesan-style cheeses and more. Just about any kind of cheese you can think of is being made in the United States from certified goat's milk, while the rest of the world has been doing this many, many years. A sudden new surge of interest in goat cheese has caused cheese sellers to sit up and take notice. Goat cheese consumption has increased both in Europe and in Canada but has skyrocketed in the United States. Sales of goat cheese are increasing faster than any segment of the cheese market in the United States, with consumption rising sharply each year. There are goat dairies in almost every state now, including Alaska and Hawaii, and the numbers continue to rise! Musty old goat milk is a thing of the past with careful attention to grazing habits and dieting. Well-tuned farming practices and equipment help the small family

milk for maintaining strong bones

farmer turn out world-class cheeses, whose tastes rival the finest imports. The taste and quality of our own domestic artisan cheeses, like our domestic wines, are fast becoming second to none. Visitors are even welcomed at most of these small family farms, which means that you can meet the goats as well as the cheese maker and buy the freshest products available on the market. You can find it fresh from a farmer near you.

While this is great news for gourmets far and wide, it also has significance for people of all ages, from babies to baby boomers, since the AMA has suggested that it's better to get your calcium from food sources than from supplements. Goat's milk may help ward off osteoporosis, as it's been recently declared superior to cow's milk for maintaining strong bones and for utilizing not only calcium but iron, phosphorous and magnesium.

Goat's milk is different from cow's milk in a couple of other important ways. Smaller fat molecules and shorter fatty acid chains result in milk that is easier to digest and can even be tolerated by some people who are lactose intolerant as well as others who are allergic to regular cow's milk. Goat's milk products are in huge demand as people discover both their delicious taste and their nutritional value. Fueled by this ever-increasing demand, grocery stores are responding by bringing in new products all the time, making both imported and domestic goat cheeses readily available to shoppers.

Whether you are cooking with cheese, looking for selections for a special cheese course or, like me, incorporating goat cheese and goat dairy in place of the cow dairy that doesn't agree with you, I hope this book will give you inspiration in the kitchen and a new appreciation for my favorite dairy food—goat cheese.

Morning Breads and Pancakes

Morning Biscuits with Chèvre and Meyer Lemon Jelly

2 cups all-purpose or whole wheat pastry flour, plus a little for kneading

1–2 tablespoons sugar

1 tablespoon baking powder

½ teaspoon baking soda

½ teaspoon salt

1 cup plain or vanilla goat yogurt

1 tablespoon butter, melted

1 tablespoon maple syrup

4 ounces chèvre or fromage blanc

Meyer Lemon Jelly or your favorite strawberry jam

This super light and airy biscuit is the perfect vehicle for chèvre and jam. In the time it takes to heat the oven, these are ready to go!

Preheat oven to 400 degrees F. In a medium bowl, combine the dry ingredients. Add the yogurt and stir until a soft ball of dough forms. Turn the dough out onto a floured surface. Knead for one minute, adding a little flour if it's too sticky. Divide the dough in half and pat each half into a small circle about 1 inch thick. With a sharp knife, cut each round into 4 wedges. Place the wedges on an ungreased cookie sheet. Melt the butter and the maple syrup together to make maple butter and brush the tops of the wedges with maple butter. Bake for 15 minutes, or until golden brown. Your nose will tell you they are ready just as the timer goes off! Serve warm with chèvre and jam or jelly.

Meyer Lemon Jelly

2 cups freshly squeezed Meyer lemon juice

2 cups sugar

1 envelope liquid fruit pectin, like Certo

4 (8-ounce) jam jars with new seals and caps

Our friend has a Meyer lemon tree. When there is a bumper crop, he brings me bucketsful.

Combine the lemon juice and sugar in a saucepan. Bring to a full rolling boil for one minute. Add the pectin, return to a boil for one full minute and then pour into clean jam jars, leaving ½ inch of head room. Set the seals, screw on the caps and quickly turn the jars over. After exactly 5 minutes, turn the jars upright again. As the jelly cools and expands over the next few hours, it will push the air out of the jars, sealing them with a little "pop!"

Farmhouse Crepes with Lemon Ricotta Filling and Roasted Cherry Jam

CREPES
1 cup fresh milk or goat milk, like Meyenberg
1 handful of ice cubes
2 tablespoons canola oil or melted butter
2 extra-large free-range eggs
1 cup flour
1 tablespoon sugar
¼ teaspoon salt

FILLING
Zest and juice of 1 Meyer lemon
⅓–½ cup sugar
4 ounces Harley Farms goat ricotta
4 ounces fromage blanc or fresh chèvre

CHERRIES
2 tablespoons butter
1 pound frozen dark cherries, pitted
⅓ cup brown sugar

If you like, you can make both the crepes and the filling in advance and have them ready in the fridge. Let things come to room temperature while you prepare the warm cherry jam. These would make a nice special occasion brunch dish or even a light dessert.

CREPES
In the carafe of the blender, combine the milk and enough ice cubes to measure a total of 1⅓ cups. Add the oil or butter and then the eggs. Blend. Combine the flour, sugar and salt in a small bowl. Add to the blender and combine until batter is smooth. Chill until needed.

FILLING
Combine the lemon zest and sugar in the food processor. Pulse until finely mixed. Add the cheeses and the lemon juice. Process until smooth. Set aside.

CHERRIES
Heat the oven to 350 degrees F. Melt the butter in a heavy skillet on the stove. Add the cherries and let them begin to thaw. Sprinkle the brown sugar over them and raise the heat, stirring. Once all the sugar has melted and the mixture begins to bubble, place the pan in the oven. Let the cherries roast for 15–20 minutes while you get everything else ready. If necessary, turn off the oven and keep the cherries inside until ready to serve.

TO COOK THE CREPES
Warm an 8-inch nonstick or crepe pan with a very light coating of cooking spray. Once the pan is hot, swirl the pan by rotating your wrist and add ¼ cup batter to the center. The batter will roll around and coat the entire pan, forming a nice thin, round crepe. After about a minute, gently flip the crepe and let it finish cooking for about 25–30 seconds. Transfer the finished crepe to a plate lined with a tea towel. Repeat with the remaining batter until you have about a dozen crepes. Keep the crepes wrapped in the towel until ready to serve.

ASSEMBLY
Set out your plates. Spoon 2–3 tablespoons of the lemon filling onto each crepe and roll up. Then spoon the hot cherry jam over the top of each, serving 2–3 per person.

Farmhouse French Toast with Camembert and Sweet Balsamic Blackberries

2   extra-large free-range eggs
1½   cups milk
½   teaspoon real vanilla extract
2   tablespoons goat butter or unsalted butter
2   tablespoons canola oil
8   thick slices day-old rustic-style sourdough, French or Italian bread
Powdered sugar, for dusting
4–6 ounces of goat Brie, Camembert or Bûcheron, sliced

Mild and creamy, soft-ripened goat cheeses take ordinary French toast into another dimension. Try a cheese from Redwood Hill or Elk Creamery. Pick fresh local berries, flash freeze them in quart ziplock bags and amaze yourself at how resourceful you are! When the cold weather sets in, you can still enjoy this little taste of summer.

Whisk the eggs, milk and vanilla together in a shallow bowl or a pie dish. Warm half the butter and oil together in a heavy skillet or on a pancake grill. Drench the bread slices, 3–4 at a time, in the milk mixture. Lift them one by one with a fork, letting the excess drip off before placing them in the hot pan. Cook them for about 3 minutes on each side over medium heat until golden brown. Repeat with the remaining butter, oil and bread slices. Dust with powdered sugar and top with the goat cheese and berries. Serve.

Sweet Balsamic Blackberries

1   pint blackberries, any variety
¼   cup honey
2   tablespoons quality balsamic vinegar

No time to make French toast? Just spoon this over your morning toast and chévre or perhaps over a bowl of vanilla yogurt!

Place a handful of the berries into a small bowl. Add the honey and balsamic vinegar, and warm for about a minute in the microwave. Mash with a fork and toss with the rest of the berries. Set aside until ready to serve.

Cherry Oatmeal Scones with Chèvre or Fromage Blanc

2½ cups all-purpose flour, plus a little more for kneading

½ cup Irish quick oats, plus a handful more for dusting the tops

1½ tablespoons baking powder

¾ teaspoon salt

½ cup unsalted butter

1 cup dried cherries, roughly chopped if large

2 tablespoons sugar

1 cup milk

1 extra-large egg white, for brushing the tops if desired

8 ounces chèvre or fromage blanc to serve with the scones

Use either sour dried cherries or sweet ones, like Bing. Dried cranberries or blueberries will also work perfectly well in place of the cherries.

Preheat oven to 400 degrees F. Mix the flour, oats, baking powder and salt in a large bowl. Slice the butter and cut it in with a wire pastry blender. Continue to work the dough until the mixture is crumbly and fine like cornmeal. (You can combine the ingredients thus far in the food processor if you prefer, but turn the mixture into a bowl at this point.) Toss the cherries in the sugar and add them to the flour mixture. Then add the milk and mix it all with a fork. Gather the dough with your hands and knead right in the bowl, adding a bit of flour only if things are too sticky.

Turn out onto a floured board. Cut the dough in half and pat each half into a circle or rectangle. Cut 6 pieces from each, ending up with 12 triangles or wedges, and place on an ungreased baking sheet.

Brush the tops with egg white and sprinkle them with oats. Bake 15 minutes, or until golden brown. Wrap in a tea towel and cool on a rack for 30 minutes before serving. Carefully cut each scone in half and spread thickly with fresh goat cheese.

Ricotta Dill Bread

1   **packet active dry yeast**

1¾ **cup warm water, not hot**

2   **tablespoons honey**

7–8 **cups all-purpose or bread
flour, like King Arthur, divided**

4   **tablespoons olive oil, divided**

¾   **cup minced yellow onion**

½   **cup finely minced fresh dill**

2   **teaspoons salt**

6   **ounces Harley Farms goat
ricotta**

1   **extra-large free-range egg**

**Egg wash (1 additional egg beaten
with a little water or milk)**

A little onion, dill and goat ricotta transform an ordinary loaf of bread. Try baking half the dough as dinner rolls, using a standard 12-cup muffin pan. If there is any bread leftover, use it the next morning for panini or toast, or make croutons for your next spinach salad!

To make the sponge, dissolve the yeast in the warm water in a large bowl. Add the honey and 2½ cups of flour. Whisk the batter until thick and smooth. Cover and let rise in a warm spot until doubled in bulk, about 45 minutes to an hour.

Warm a tablespoon of oil in a small saucepan over a medium low flame. Add the onion and cook slowly until softened. Add the dill and the salt, and remove from the heat. Crumble the ricotta into the onion/dill mixture. Work in with a fork until the ricotta is thoroughly incorporated.

When the sponge has doubled, add the ricotta mixture, the eggs and the remaining oil, and stir it down. Add another 4–5 cups of flour, ½ cup at a time. Enough flour has been added once the dough is no longer sticky but smooth and elastic. Turn the dough out onto a floured work surface and knead for another 5 minutes, adding a little more flour if necessary to keep the dough from sticking to the board. Transfer the dough to an oiled bowl. Flip the dough over so the top is oiled. Cover and let rise in a warm spot until doubled in volume.

Turn out onto the floured work surface. Punch down the dough, divide and shape into two loaves. Place the dough into 2 oiled bread pans, pressing the dough into the corners with a closed fist to push out any excess air. Let rise one final time. Preheat oven to 350 degrees F. Brush the tops of the loaves with the egg wash just before popping them into the hot oven.

Bake the loaves for 45–50 minutes, until golden brown. Remove from the pans and cool on racks. Cool completely before slicing.

Sweet Ricotta Pancakes with Bananas and Strawberries

8	ounces Harley Farms goat ricotta
1	large or 2 small very ripe bananas, mashed
1	teaspoon vanilla
4	extra-large egg whites, beaten stiff, divided
1	cup flour
2	tablespoons sugar
1	teaspoon cinnamon
1½	teaspoons baking powder
¼	teaspoon salt
½	cup canola oil, for frying
	Powdered sugar or cinnamon sugar, for dusting
1 or 2	pints of fresh ripe strawberries

These little pancakes remind me of the beignets we had long ago when my husband and I visited New Orleans. My version falls somewhere between a pancake and a doughnut, and makes a really easy but festive morning treat for company.

With a fork or an electric mixer, combine the ricotta, banana, vanilla and about half the beaten egg whites in a medium bowl. Don't worry if it's a bit lumpy. Combine the dry ingredients and add to the ricotta mixture, stirring until just mixed. Fold in the remaining egg whites.

Warm the oil in a heavy skillet until hot but not smoking. Drop the batter by tablespoonfuls into the hot oil, doing 4–6 at a time. Carefully flip them over when medium golden-brown and cook the other side. Remove to a plate lined with paper towels. Repeat with the rest of the batter. Roll them in a little powdered sugar or cinnamon sugar, top with strawberries and serve as soon as possible.

Espresso Ginger Cakes with Chèvre and Bodega Dairy Caramel

¾   cup very strong hot coffee or
      espresso
½   cup dark unsulfured molasses
1   teaspoon baking soda
2   ounces crystallized ginger
½   cup brown sugar
⅓   cup canola oil
1   extra-large free-range egg
1½ cups all-purpose flour
1   teaspoon cinnamon
½   teaspoon salt
1   pinch ground cloves
4–6 ounces fresh chèvre or from-
      age blanc
1   (4-ounce) tub Bodega Natilla

This recipe couldn't be easier—a dark springy muffin that is light and not overly sweet. I had meant to simply serve it with fromage blanc but stumbled on my little tubs of caramel in the fridge that I had bought at the Sonoma Cheese Festival. The subtle combination of ginger, espresso and caramel along with the creamy fromage blanc works perfectly! I have included the telephone number for the caramel in Resources (page 136). It's a *dulce de leche*, or soft caramel, made from goat's milk in the traditional Peruvian style by Bodega and Yerba Santa Goat Dairy. You can bake this batter as an 8 x 8-inch gingerbread and spread the caramel like icing!

Preheat oven to 350 degrees F. Warm the coffee and molasses in a medium saucepan or in a quart-size glass measuring cup in the microwave for about a minute. Whisk in the baking soda (it will react and bubble up). Stir it down and set aside to cool.

Finely mince the ginger with the sugar in a mini chop or food processor. Transfer the ginger-sugar mixture to a medium mixing bowl and add the canola oil and egg. Whisk until creamy.

Combine the dry ingredients separately. Add half of this mixture and half of the coffee mixture to the ginger-sugar mixture until just combined. Repeat with the remaining ingredients. Pour into oiled, standard-size muffin tins. Bake for 15–18 minutes, or until the tops spring back.

Cool in the pan for 10 minutes before removing. Serve with chèvre and caramel.

Blueberry Morning Tarts

1½ cups whole wheat pastry
flour, like Bob's Red Mill

3 tablespoons powdered sugar

½ teaspoon salt

6 tablespoons cold unsalted
butter

3–4 tablespoons ice water

2 extra-large free-range eggs

4 ounces Harley Farms ricotta
or fromage blanc

⅓ cup honey

1 teaspoon vanilla

3 cups blueberries, fresh or
frozen (frozen will work just
fine—don't thaw them!),
divided

¼ cup orange marmalade

These tasty little tarts are wonderful for breakfast or teatime, as they are not too heavy or too sweet. You can, however, splurge and top them with vanilla gelato for dessert!

Combine the flour, sugar and salt in a medium bowl. Slice the butter and cut it into the flour with a pastry blender until crumbly. Add ice water a tablespoon at a time, mixing with a fork. When the dough is moist enough to form a ball, turn out onto a floured surface. Knead a bit until it's no longer sticky. Roll out and cut into twelve 3-inch circles. Invert a muffin tin and push the 12 circles onto the pan, forming 12 little upside-down tart shells. Freeze upside down like that for at least 30 minutes.

Bake at 400 degrees F, still upside down, for about 15 minutes. Cool slightly. Turn the oven down to 325 degrees F. Lift the shells carefully off the muffin tin and place right side up on a cookie sheet.

In a small bowl, whisk together the eggs, ricotta, honey and vanilla. Add 1 cup of the berries and gently stir. Spoon the mixture into the tart shells. Bake until slightly puffy and beginning to set up and brown, about 25–30 minutes. Let cool.

Warm the marmalade in a small saucepan and stir in the remaining berries. Let cool. Top the tarts with the berries just before serving.

Frittatas, Omelettes and Eggs

Sunburst Frittata with Ricotta, Cilantro and Jalapeño

1 pound green and yellow zucchini or Sunburst squash, grated

1 teaspoon salt

1–2 jalapeño peppers, sliced into thin rings

2 tablespoons plus 1 teaspoon olive oil, divided

1/2 cup packed cilantro leaves

1–2 garlic cloves

2 smallish yellow zucchini or Sunburst squash, reserved for top

5–6 extra-large free-range eggs

2 tablespoons butter, divided

4 ounces Harley Farms ricotta or fresh chèvre, or a mixture of the two

You can skip the fancy top on this, if you like. Just leave out the two Sunburst squash for the top and scatter the jalapeño slices over the top instead.

Toss the grated zucchini and salt together in a bowl. Transfer to a fine strainer set over the bowl and let drain for about 30 minutes. Rinse and drain the grated zucchini and roll in a clean kitchen towel to remove the moisture.

Preheat the broiler. Sauté the jalapeños in 1 teaspoon olive oil in a small pan for 1 or 2 minutes on each side to mellow the flavor and soften them a bit. Then finely mince any leftover jalapeño with the cilantro and garlic, and set aside. You need 9 or 10 jalapeño rings for the center garnish.

Prepare the sunburst for the top by slicing the reserved yellow squash thinly at an angle so that each slice looks like a flower petal. Arrange the slices on a dinner plate to create a pattern. Cover with plastic wrap and microwave for about a minute to partially cook.

Crack the eggs into a medium bowl and whisk in a tablespoon of water.

In a wide skillet or omelette pan, melt 1 tablespoon each of butter and olive oil. Add the zucchini and sauté for 4 or 5 minutes, until soft. Add the minced jalapeños, cilantro and garlic. Cook one more minute and then cool a bit. Add to the bowl of eggs.

Soften the ricotta in a small bowl in the microwave for about 30 seconds. If you are using chèvre, there is no need to warm and soften it. Set the cheese aside for now.

Wipe the pan clean and place it over medium heat. Add the remaining tablespoons of butter and oil, being careful not to burn the butter. As soon as the pan is piping hot, pour in the egg mixture. Rotate the pan a little to distribute the eggs evenly. Then turn the flame down to low and let it cook for about 2 minutes.

Working quickly, scatter the ricotta and/or chèvre over the eggs. Arrange sliced squash over the top in a sunburst pattern, or simply spread them evenly on top. When the frittata looks partially set (edges will look cooked but center will be gooey at this point), turn off the flame and cover. Let it set for 2–3 minutes, and then uncover and place it under the broiler to finish. A couple of minutes under the broiler will be plenty, so stay close and keep an eye on it. Remove it from the heat as soon as it appears to be set in the center. Let rest a few minutes before serving.

Farmhouse Eggs with Tomatoes, Black Beans and Cheddar

1 tablespoon olive oil

1 tablespoon butter

1 large sweet onion, diced

1 (15-ounce) can diced organic tomatoes or 2 cups diced fresh tomatoes

2 (15-ounce) cans black beans, drained

4 flour tortillas

4 extra-large free-range eggs

4 ounces goat cheddar, grated

½ cup plain yogurt cheese (page 76), fromage blanc or sour cream

Chopped green onions and cilantro, for garnish

This dish is just as much at home at dinnertime as it is at breakfast or brunch. You can make it with canned black beans, which I always keep in the pantry for this, or you can make your own black beans from scratch. If I have any homemade black bean chili leftovers, I use those instead! Use fresh tomatoes when they are in season and canned diced organic tomatoes the rest of the year. Rumiano raw milk cheddar, Hillman Harvest cheddar or Le Chèvre Noir, an amazing aged cheddar from Canada, would all be great choices for the cheese.

Preheat oven or broiler, as you will need to melt the cheese quickly just before serving.

Warm the olive oil and butter in a large skillet or paella pan. Add the onion and sauté slowly until soft. Add the tomatoes and let stew for a good 10 minutes or so, until the juices are a beautiful orangey color.

Meanwhile, warm the black beans in a small saucepan. Wrap the tortillas in a clean, damp dish towel and microwave for 1 minute to warm and soften them.

Carefully crack the eggs, one at a time, and set them on top of the simmering tomatoes. Turn the heat down to low and cover the pan. When the eggs are just set on the top, assemble the individual servings. On each plate, tuck a poached egg with some of the tomatoes into each tortilla and fold closed. Smother with a spoonful of beans and sprinkle with a generous handful of grated cheddar. Place under the broiler just long enough to melt the cheese. Serve with a dollop of yogurt cheese and a sprinkling of green onions and cilantro. Pass the hot sauce!

Portabella Mushroom Frittata with Herbs and Aged Gouda

12-ounces portabella mushrooms, (crimini or button), cleaned and sliced

1   medium red onion, sliced and quartered

¼   cup sliced sun-dried tomatoes, packed in olive oil

2   tablespoons finely sliced fresh sage, thyme, oregano or basil

6–8 extra-large free-range eggs

1   tablespoon water

1   tablespoon olive oil

1   tablespoon butter

2–4 ounces goat Gouda, grated

Try using Cypress Grove's Midnight Moon for this recipe or use a younger, creamier Gouda like Arina or Chèvre brand. If you are using a well-aged, 2–3 ounces should be plenty. Use a little more if using a younger cheese—3–4 ounces. Sweet Potato Fries (page 96) and a simple spinach salad make great brunch or dinner companions for this frittata!

Preheat broiler or warm oven to 450 degrees F. In a heavy skillet, combine the mushrooms, onions and tomatoes, along with the oil the tomatoes are packed in. Cook over medium heat until the mushrooms are a lovely dark brown, about 15 minutes, adding the herbs in the last few minutes. Remove from heat and cool a minute or two.

Beat the eggs in a medium bowl with water. Spoon the mushroom mixture into the eggs. Stir gently. Wipe the skillet clean, turn the heat to medium-high and add the olive oil and butter.

When the butter is melted and foamy, add the egg mixture. Rotate the pan to evenly distribute the ingredients. Reduce the heat to low and cook until the outer part of the frittata is beginning to set, about 2–3 minutes. The center will still be gooey at this point. Arrange the cheese on top of the frittata and place under the broiler for a minute or two, watching carefully so as not to overcook the eggs. Once the cheese is nicely melted, remove from oven. Let rest a few minutes before serving or let sit a while—it tastes great at room temperature, too.

Naked Omelette with Canadian Bacon and Scallions

1   teaspoon olive oil

1–2 scallions, finely diced

¼   cup finely diced Canadian
    bacon

2   eggs, beaten with 1 or 2
    teaspoons water

1   ounce hard goat cheese,
    grated

This is the simplest of omelettes, almost like the skinny kind you might get for lunch in a Paris café. Five minutes from start to finish. This one calls for Naked Goat, which is a manchego-style cheese from Spain, but you can use anything that will grate.

Oil an omelette pan and set it over medium-high heat. Toss in scallions and Canadian bacon, stirring them to mix. Once they have heated through and are beginning to sizzle, add the eggs and rotate the pan to distribute them evenly. Lower the heat and watch carefully. In a minute or so, the eggs will be almost set. At this point, scatter the grated cheese over them. As soon as the cheese is almost melted, remove the pan from the heat. The heat from the pan will finish cooking the center of the omelette in no time. As soon as the center is set, fold both sides toward the middle, ending up with the omelette folded in thirds. Slip onto a plate and serve immediately.

Curried Crab Pancakes with Chèvre and Quick Tomato and Apple Chutney

4 tablespoons olive oil, divided
1 large onion, chopped
1 cup very finely diced red potato
6–8 cloves garlic, minced
2 tablespoons freshly minced ginger
1–2 jalapeños, seeded and minced
1 tablespoon curry powder (I like Morton & Bassett)
1 tablespoon yellow mustard seeds
1/2 pound freshly cracked crabmeat
4 extra-large free-range eggs
2 tablespoons butter, divided
4 ounces chèvre
Quick Tomato and Apple Chutney (page 70)

As a change from the usual omelette or frittata presentation, I decided to play with the mixture and make individual mini frittatas or "pancakes" instead of one big one. For this, you can use a frying pan and make 3 or 4 at a time or use a pancake grill. Add a side of Roasted Asparagus (page 98) and maybe some jasmine rice for a really nice light supper.

Warm 2 tablespoons oil in a large skillet over medium heat and add the onion. Stir to coat with oil and add the potato. Cook until soft, about 5 minutes. Add the garlic, ginger and jalapeño. After about a minute, add the curry and mustard seed, and stir thoroughly. Gently stir in the crab and cook until completely heated through. Remove from the heat.

Beat the eggs in a medium bowl and stir in the slightly cooled crab mixture.

Wipe out the skillet and add 1 tablespoon oil and 1 tablespoon butter. Once the pan is nice and hot, add the batter with a large spoon, using about 1/3 cup batter per pancake. When the pancakes are set and lightly brown on the bottom, flip with a large spatula. Keep warm on a plate in the oven while cooking the remaining batter, adding the remaining oil and butter to the pan, if needed. Serve as soon as possible, topped with some of the chèvre and chutney.

Rainbow Chard Omelette with Crispy Cumin-and-Ginger Potatoes

½ red onion, thinly sliced

2 tablespoons olive oil, divided

1 bunch fresh rainbow chard or spinach, washed, stemmed and sliced

Salt and pepper to taste

1 tablespoon butter

4 extra-large free-range eggs, whisked together in a medium bowl with 1 tablespoon water

3 ounces sliced or crumbled goat cheese

Any favorite goat cheese will finish off this omelette. Slices of creamy semisoft cheese like a young Jack or Gouda would melt really well. Crumbly feta or blue would be really flavorful with the chard, or you could dice up that leftover Brie or Humboldt Fog you have in the fridge from the night before! I don't think there's a bad choice to be made here.

In an omelette pan or skillet, sauté the onion in 1 tablespoon of olive oil. Once the onions are soft, add the chard or spinach. Cook the leaves for several minutes until they shrink down and become limp. Scrape them onto a small dish, salt and pepper to taste and set aside.

Wipe out the omelette pan and return it to the stove. Warm the pan and add the tablespoon of butter and remaining olive oil. Rotate the pan to combine them; when they are siz-zling hot, add the beaten eggs. Swirl the pan to evenly distribute the eggs; turn the heat down to low. When the eggs are just about set, spread the cooked chard on one side of the omelette and sprinkle with goat cheese. Turn off the heat. After about a minute, close the omelette by folding it in half with a large spatula and gently slide it onto a warm serving plate next to a generous helping of potatoes.

Crispy Cumin-and-Ginger Potatoes

3–4 tablespoons canola or olive oil

1½ pounds red creamer potatoes, cut in small bite-size wedges

1 tablespoon whole cumin seed

1 tablespoon ground cumin

1 teaspoon mustard seed

2 tablespoons freshly grated ginger

6–8 cloves garlic, minced

½ teaspoon salt

Serve these potatoes as a side for the Rainbow Chard Omelette or the Farmhouse Eggs with Black Beans (page 41). The kitchen will fill with the amazing aroma of the spices, announcing that breakfast is almost ready.

Warm a large skillet over medium heat. Add the oil and rotate the pan to coat. Add the potatoes to the hot oil and let them brown a few minutes on each side, about 10 minutes altogether. At this point, add the cumin seed, ground cumin and mustard seed, and toss to coat. Then add the ginger, garlic and salt. Let the potatoes continue to cook slowly for another 10 minutes or so while preparing the omelette.

Lemon Breakfast Tart

8 ounces fresh chèvre

8 ounces fresh goat ricotta

4 extra-large free-range eggs

²/₃ cup plus 2 tablespoons sugar, divided

¹/₄ cup freshly squeezed lemon juice

1 tablespoon lemon zest

1 (9-inch) pre-baked or home-made deep fluted tart shell

Powdered sugar, for dusting

Serve this lightly sweetened cheesecake-style tart for breakfast, teatime or a special-occasion brunch. For the tart dough, use the one from the Bartlett Pear Tart (page 125) or try the whole-wheat pastry flour crust from the Blueberry Morning Tarts (page 28). Use a deep 9-inch fluted tart pan with a removable bottom or opt for two smaller more shallow tart pans, which will cook a bit faster. A fresh fruit salad would be the perfect complement to this tart.

Preheat oven to 350 degrees F.

Place the chèvre, ricotta, eggs, 2/3 cup sugar and lemon juice in the blender or standing mixer. Finely mince the lemon zest in a mini chop with the 2 tablespoons sugar. Add the lemon-sugar mixture to the chèvre mixture and combine. When smooth, pour into the tart shell, place on a cookie sheet and bake about 45 minutes, or until puffy and set in the center. (Bake 25 minutes if using 2 very shallow tart pans instead of 1 deep one.) Toward the end of bake time, the top of the tart may crack a bit but will settle back down into place after cooling.

Cool on a wire rack. Dust with powdered sugar and serve at room temperature.

LEMON-ARTICHOKE VARIATION

For a savory version of this tart, omit the sugar entirely and add 1 (15-ounce) can drained artichoke hearts, 1 peeled clove of garlic and 1 tablespoon of capers to the blender mixture. Before baking as directed, top the tart with sliced tricolor mini bell peppers.

Pizzas and Quesadillas

Cornmeal Pizza Dough

1   cup warm water (very warm—
     like bathwater!)

1¼   teaspoons active dry yeast,
     about ½ packet

½   teaspoon sugar or honey

2   tablespoons olive oil

3   cups all-purpose or bread flour,
     plus a little more for kneading

¼   cup coarse cornmeal, plus 1
     tablespoon for each baking
     sheet

1   teaspoon salt

Once you get the hang of making fresh pizza dough, you can create just about any kind of pizza you can think of. Here are just a few simple pizzas to spring from. I really like a little cornmeal in my pizza dough. It gives the dough a little color and heft, and adds just a touch of earthiness. You can simply omit it if you want to.

This recipe makes enough for 4 as a main course but is easily doubled. Store extra dough in the fridge for several days or freeze for up to a month. Cut the dough into useable pieces, wrap them in plastic wrap and then slip them into a ziplock bag for safekeeping. Always let refrigerated dough sit out for 20 minutes or more before working with it. Thaw frozen dough in the fridge overnight for best results.

DOUGH

Place the warm water, yeast and sugar or honey in a large mixing bowl. Whisk together and let stand 10 minutes to dissolve and activate the yeast. The surface will begin to appear foamy and then you will know that your yeast is awake! Add the olive oil and stir. Combine the flour, cornmeal and salt, and add to the liquid, stirring to blend with a wooden spoon. The dough will begin to come together into a ball.

Turn the dough out onto a work surface sprinkled with a little more flour. Knead the dough, adding a touch of flour if necessary to keep the dough from sticking. In about 5–10 minutes, the dough should be soft and pliable. Place it in an oiled bowl and then flip the dough once to oil the top side. Cover with plastic wrap and let rise in a warm spot until doubled or close to tripled in volume, about 1½ hours.

PIZZA ASSEMBLY

Preheat oven to 450 degrees F. When the dough is ready, punch it down to get rid of all the air inside. Cut the dough in fourths or in half, depending what size pizzas you would like. Wrap up any pieces you aren't using immediately and store in the fridge or freezer for another time.

Roll out the dough into thin rounds. Sprinkle cookie sheet(s) with the cornmeal. To transfer the dough to the baking sheet, carefully fold the dough in half, pick it up and open it again on top of the cornmeal. The cornmeal keeps it from sticking to the cookie sheets. Proceed with selected toppings and bake as directed in each individual recipe.

Pesto Pizza

2	cups packed basil leaves
2	cloves garlic
1/3	cup pine nuts
1/2	cup olive oil
1/2	teaspoon salt
1	recipe cornmeal pizza dough
8	ounces goat mozzarella

Making fresh pesto takes less than 5 minutes. This pizza has maximum flavor for minimum effort!

Preheat oven to 450 degrees F. Combine the basil, garlic, pine nuts, oil and salt in the food processor or blender until almost smooth. Don't over blend it—a little texture is preferable. Spoon the pesto over the prepared pizza dough and top with sliced mozzarella. Bake for about 15 minutes, or until the crust is lightly browned on the edges. Cool a few moments before slicing and serving.

Pizza Margarita

1 recipe cornmeal pizza dough
2 tablespoons olive oil
1 pound Roma tomatoes, sliced
   and seeded, or about 2 cups
   pizza sauce
8 ounces goat mozzarella,
   sliced
4–6 cloves garlic, chopped
1/2 cup sliced basil
Freshly ground pepper, optional

This is the simplest of pizzas—just cheese and tomato with a little basil and garlic. When in season, you can use fresh sliced tomatoes. The rest of the year, use a pizza sauce instead. See the Quick Tomato Pizza Sauce below. If you can't find goat mozzarella locally, have some shipped from Fraga Farms!

Preheat oven to 450 degrees F. Brush the prepared dough with olive oil.

Cut tomatoes in half crosswise, and squeeze out and discard the seeds. Slice and spread tomatoes or spoon out sauce, if using, leaving an inch around the edge. Arrange the cheese slices on top and sprinkle with garlic and basil. (If you want your tomatoes on top of the cheese, please do it that way! If you don't want your basil crispy,

put it on in the last few minutes of baking or after you remove the pizza from the oven). If you like, grind some fresh pepper and drizzle a little more olive oil over the top.

Bake the pizza for 15 minutes, or until golden brown around the edges. Transfer to a pizza peel or cutting board. Let rest a few minutes before slicing.

Quick Tomato Pizza Sauce

1/2 cup finely diced onion
2 cloves garlic, minced
2 tablespoons olive oil
1 (15-ounce) can organic fire-
   roasted or plum tomatoes,
   drained
2 tablespoons tomato paste
   (optional)

Don't have any pizza sauce? Make your own. It'll taste better anyway. This sauce comes together in less than 10 minutes.

Sauté the onion and garlic in olive oil. Cool a bit and transfer to the food processor. Add the tomatoes and pulse until smooth. Add tomato paste if you like your sauce thicker.

Cornmeal Pizza with Chèvre, Sun-Dried Tomatoes and Basil

3–4 cloves garlic or shallots, sliced or chopped

¼ cup olive oil

½ recipe pizza dough

½ cup sliced sun-dried tomatoes, oil packed

1 zucchini, sliced and cooked (optional)

1 chicken breast, diced and cooked (optional)

4 ounces chèvre

½ cup sliced fresh basil leaves

This pizza is a favorite in my house. We also like it with diced chicken or sliced zucchini that's been quickly browned beforehand with the garlic and olive oil. I like to make this pizza with a half recipe of dough, and then I make a Pesto or a Margarita pizza with the other half.

Preheat oven to 450 degrees F. Combine garlic or shallots and olive oil in a small bowl and warm in the microwave for 1 minute. Then spread evenly over the dough, leaving an inch around the edges. Add the sun-dried tomatoes and the zucchini or chicken, if using. Bake for about 12 minutes. Quickly top with the chèvre and basil, and return to the oven for 3–5 minutes. Cool briefly before slicing.

Tiny Pizzas with Oven-Roasted Tomatoes and Brie

⅓ cup olive oil

3–4 cloves garlic, minced

8–10 ounces well-chilled goat Brie
  or Camembert

½ recipe cornmeal pizza dough

18–24 ready-made oven-roasted
  tomato halves or make the
  Oven-Roasted Tomatoes below

1 handful basil leaves, thinly sliced

Kosher or sea salt

OVEN-ROASTED TOMATOES

12 Roma tomatoes, halved and
  seeded

Olive oil, for brushing

1 teaspoon sugar

If you don't have time to oven roast your own tomatoes, you can sometimes find ready-made ones next to the olives in the gourmet grocer's cheese or deli section. Goat Brie tastes great but melts fast, so keep an eye on the pizzas in the oven so the cheese doesn't melt away!

Let pizza dough sit out for 20 minutes while preparing the other ingredients.

Preheat oven to 425 degrees F. Combine the olive oil and garlic in a glass measuring cup. Warm in the microwave for a minute or so to flavor the oil. Set aside. Slice cheese into ¼-inch-thick slices that will end up being about 1 x 2 inches to fit on top of the little pizzas.

Cut pizza dough into 18–24 pieces about the size of a cherry tomato. On a floured work surface, roll or flatten each piece into a circle about 2½ inches around. Place them on a parchment-lined baking sheet, brush with garlic oil and pre-bake for 6–8 minutes until lightly coloring around the edges. Remove from oven but leave oven on.

Top pizzas with a slice of cheese and a tomato half. Put the sliced basil into remaining garlic oil in the sauté pan to coat. Sprinkle a little basil, oil mixture and salt on each tomato. Return to the oven for a few minutes, just long enough to melt the cheese. Serve warm or at room temperature.

OVEN-ROASTED TOMATOES

Place the tomato halves, cut side up, on a cookie sheet and brush with olive oil. Put sugar in the palm of your hand and sprinkle over the tomatoes. Bake at 250–275 degrees F for a couple hours until the tomatoes are flattened down a bit and very fragrant. You can prepare them in advance and keep in the fridge.

Portabella Mushroom Pizza

3–4 cloves garlic, chopped

2   tablespoons fresh thyme leaves, chopped

⅓   cup olive oil

½   recipe pizza dough

½   cup seeded and chopped Roma tomatoes

4   ounces crimini or portabella mushrooms, sliced

½   red bell pepper, sliced or diced

½   yellow bell pepper, sliced or diced

2   shallots, sliced

4   ounces chèvre or slices of a soft-ripened Brie-style cheese

Freshly ground pepper

What is it about these giant mushrooms that I can't get enough of? When I was a kid, I used to love sausage-and-mushroom pizza best. Now I like my mushroom pizza veggie-style with crumbled chèvre and lots of thyme and garlic!

Combine the garlic, thyme and olive oil in a small heat-proof bowl and microwave for 1 minute. Spread over the dough. Then spread with tomatoes, mushrooms, bell peppers, shallots and the chèvre, leaving an inch of bare crust. Grind fresh pepper over the top. Bake for 12 minutes, or until lightly brown and irresistible looking! Cool a moment before slicing.

Portabella Mushroom Quesadillas with Thyme and Goat Jack

8   ounces portabella mushrooms, sliced

3–4 cloves garlic, minced

1   tablespoon freshly minced thyme leaves

2–3 tablespoons extra virgin olive oil

1   tablespoon balsamic vinegar

1   tablespoon soy sauce

4   (8-inch) flour tortillas

A little butter or olive oil, for the skillet

3–4 ounces grated semisoft goat cheese

Whole Foods Markets carry a nice selection of goat Jacks, cheddars and Goudas that are readily available and perfect for quesadillas. For a rosemary version, omit the thyme and use Cabra Romero, a luscious creamy Spanish semisoft cheese crusted with rosemary!

Sauté the mushrooms, garlic and thyme in olive oil until mushrooms are nicely browned. Season with vinegar and soy sauce. Turn up the heat to boil off any excess liquids and then remove from heat.

Place one tortilla in a warm, lightly buttered skillet. Spread on half the cheese and half the mushrooms, and top with another tortilla.

Press down gently with the flat of your hand to encourage the melting cheese to bind the tortillas together. When nicely browned on the bottom, carefully flip and brown the other side. By now the cheese inside should be gooey and melted. Remove to a cutting board and repeat with remaining ingredients. Cut in quarters and serve immediately.

Chicken Quesadillas with Green Olives and Manchego

A little butter or oil for the skillet

4   (8-inch) flour tortillas

3–4 ounces grated manchego-
     style goat, Naked Goat, ched-
     dar, Gouda, etc.

2   cups shredded, cooked
     chicken

²/₃ cup sliced green olives or
     green olive tapenade

You can find manchego made from goat's milk if you know where to look, but you can substitute any semisoft melting cheese for this recipe. Some cheeses that are very similar to manchego are Naked Goat, Iberico, Monteban, Garrotxa and Majorero. Goat Jack, Goat Gouda, Goat Cheddar, Drunken Goat, Queso de Cabra—any of these will be great with the chicken and olives. When I am in a hurry, I use green olive tapenade from a jar—a ten-minute wonder if you have leftover chicken!

Place one tortilla in a warm, lightly buttered skillet. Spread on half the cheese, half the chicken and half the olives, and top with another tortilla. Press down gently with the flat of your hand to encourage the melting cheese to bind the tortillas together. When nicely browned on the bottom, carefully flip and brown the other side. By now the cheese inside should be gooey and melted. Remove to a cutting board and repeat with remaining ingredients. Cool a moment or so and then cut into quarters and serve.

Appetizers and Sandwiches

Bruschetta with Olive Oil and Herbs

2–3 cloves garlic

⅓ cup olive oil

2 French baguettes, sliced on the diagonal

2–3 tablespoons finely minced fresh herbs, such as oregano and rosemary

2–3 varieties of goat cheese

One or more toppings as listed

Crispy olive oil toast with goat cheese and toppings makes for a perfect party atmosphere. You can assemble them as hors d'oeuvres or simply leave ingredients out for guests to serve themselves. Any single goat cheese or an assortment of your favorite cheeses and toppings works with this bruschetta as a willing vehicle. Figure 2–3 ounces of goat cheese per person—a little less if you are having a big meal afterward. Soft fresh cheeses like chèvre, feta and mozzarella as well as soft, ripened cheeses from the Brie family are natural companions for the toppings below. Add an aged cheese to your assortment for contrast: a semisoft like Drunken Goat or the rosemary-crusted Cabra Romero. A well-aged goat cheese like Cabra Pimento or the new Cabralinda from Nicolau Farms in Modesto would be firm enough to shave very thin. Don't forget the olives!

Preheat oven to 400 degrees F (or heat a stovetop grill, if you prefer). Slice the garlic and combine with oil in a glass measuring cup. Warm in the microwave a minute to flavor the oil. Brush the baguette slices lightly with the oil. If you are doing them in the oven, put the oil side up; on the grill, put the oil side down. When the bread is browned to your liking, remove from the heat and arrange on a platter. Sprinkle with the herbs and serve with assorted cheeses and one or more of these toppings: Roasted Red Pepper Tapenade, Christmas Lima Bean Dip or Fresh Tomato Tapenade.

Roasted Red Pepper Tapenade

¼ cup extra virgin olive oil

1 medium onion, diced

3–4 cloves garlic, sliced

2 freshly roasted red bell pepper, skinned, or a couple of jarred peppers

4 ounces sliced sun-dried tomatoes, oil packed

1–2 ounce anchovy fillets, optional

Red pepper flakes, if you want it spicy

2 tablespoons capers

Salt and freshly ground pepper to taste

The anchovies will add a little saltiness to this spread, so be sure to taste the tapenade before adding any more salt. It should be only mildly salty, as both the cheese and the bread are salty on their own. If you are not an anchovy fan, simply leave them out.

Warm the olive oil and sauté the onions in it until soft. Add the garlic for one minute. Cool. Transfer to a food processor and add the bell peppers, tomatoes and anchovies. Season with red pepper flakes and freshly ground pepper, if desired. Pulse to combine but don't overdo it; it should be a little chunky. Spoon into a serving dish and stir in the capers. Taste before you add salt and pepper.

Spinach and Feta Triangles

1 **medium red onion, minced**
2 **tablespoons olive oil**
6–8 **cloves garlic, minced**
1 **(8–10 ounce) bag frozen spinach**
4 **ounces feta**
Zest of 1 lemon
¼ **teaspoon grated nutmeg**
Salt and pepper to taste
1 **box puff pastry dough, thawed in the fridge**

Spinach and goat cheese just seem to have been made for one another. These triangles are an easy make-ahead item for a party or just something special to enjoy with a glass of good Chardonnay. For about an hour's worth of preparation, you can have these waiting in the freezer, ready to be baked at a moment's notice.

Sauté the onion in olive oil until soft, about 5 minutes. Add the garlic and then the spinach. Stir to mix and sauté long enough to cook away any excess water. Turn off the heat and let cool a bit.

Crumble the feta in a medium bowl. Add the cooled spinach mixture, lemon zest and nutmeg. Salt and pepper to taste. Cover and chill for at least an hour.

Meanwhile, remove the puff pastry from the freezer and unfold. Cut the dough in half length-wise, rewrap half of it and return to the fridge while working with the other half. You don't want it at room temperature.

On a lightly floured cutting board, cut the remaining dough in half again crosswise, forming 2 squares. Working quickly, roll out each piece until you have 2 rectangles about 8 x 12 inches. Cut each into 6 squares, leaving 12 squares approximately 4 x 4 inches. Place a heaping tablespoon of the chilled filling in the center of each square and fold corner to corner, forming little triangles. Press edges together so the filling won't escape, and flash freeze on an open plate for about 15–20 minutes. Repeat process with the other half of refrigerated dough.

Preheat oven to 400 degrees F. Bake for 15 minutes, or until nicely golden brown, or place in a freezer bag to be baked at a later time. They should go straight from the freezer into the pre-heated oven. Don't thaw them! These will keep nicely in the freezer for weeks.

Crispy Olive Oil Crackers

2 **cups all-purpose flour, plus ¼ cup for rolling**
1 **teaspoon baking powder**
1 **teaspoon salt**
1 **teaspoon sugar**
¼ **cup water**
¼ **cup olive oil**

Here is a very simple recipe for delicious homemade crackers. They can be made a few days in advance or while your torte (page 64) is chilling.

Preheat oven to 325 degrees F. Combine the dry ingredients in a bowl. Add the water and olive oil, and work into a ball of dough. Divide the dough in half. Set one aside and roll the other out to about ⅛ inch thick, dusting with extra flour to keep dough from sticking to the work surface. Carefully cut into triangles and transfer to a parchment-lined baking sheet. Bake 15–20 minutes, or until the crackers turn golden brown. Remove from baking sheet and cool. Repeat with remaining dough. Serve with either torte on page 64 or with soft chèvre and Roasted Red Pepper Tapenade (page 60).

Layered Pesto, Chèvre and Tomato Torte with Pine Nuts

TORTE
10–12 ounces fresh chèvre
1 cup packed basil leaves
¼ cup extra virgin olive oil
1 clove garlic
⅓ cup pine nuts
½ teaspoon salt
½ pint small red and yellow
　　cherry tomatoes, cut into
　　quarters
1 roasted red bell pepper, finely
　　diced

ANCHO CHILE PUREE & ACHIOTE OIL
2 ounces dried ancho chiles,
　　stemmed and seeded
2 small clean jam jars
1 cup olive oil
2 tablespoons annatto seeds

You can make this torte with a traditional basil pesto and top with tomatoes and roasted bell peppers or prepare it using cilantro in place of the basil. The cilantro version is fantastic with ancho chile puree on top, but if you don't have time to make it up, just spoon some salsa over it instead. Either way, a little achiote oil adds a nice finishing touch!

TORTE
Line a 5- or 6-inch springform pan or a soup plate with plastic wrap, leaving enough extra wrap on either side for covering up afterwards. Press half the chèvre into the bottom using the back of a spoon.

Combine the basil, olive oil, garlic, half of the pine nuts and salt in the food processor or mini chop and pulse to combine. Spoon this thick pesto mixture over the chèvre. Top with the rest of the chèvre and press gently with the back of the spoon to smooth into place. Wrap tightly and chill for at least an hour and up to 24 hours.

When ready to serve, unmold and top the torte with the tomatoes, peppers and a drizzle of the achiote oil. Garnish with the remaining pine nuts and serve with the Bruschetta (page 60).

CILANTRO AND PUMPKIN SEED VARIATION
Prepare the torte as above, using cilantro in place of the basil and pumpkin seeds in place of the pine nuts. When ready to serve, unmold onto a plate. Spread chile puree over the top and drizzle with achiote oil. Sprinkle with toasted pumpkin seeds and serve with thick organic tortilla chips or Crispy Olive Oil Crackers (page 62).

ANCHO CHILE PUREE
Bake chiles in the oven for 5 minutes at 325 degrees F. Place in a bowl and cover with boiling water. Soak for about 20 minutes, drain and puree in the food processor. Spoon the puree into a small jam jar.

ACHIOTE OIL
While the chiles are soaking, warm the olive oil and annatto seeds together in a small saucepan or in the microwave. As it comes to a simmer, you will see the red color weeping into the oil. Remove from heat and cool for at least half an hour. Strain the orange-colored oil into the second jar, discarding the seeds.

Fresh Tomato Tapenade

1   **pound fresh ripe tomatoes, seeded and chopped**
2   **cloves garlic, minced and poached in ¼ cup extra virgin olive oil for 1 minute**
¼   **cup chopped pitted kalamata olives**
1   **tablespoon capers**
¼   **cup chopped basil**
3   **ounces crumbled goat feta**
Salt and pepper to taste

Organic Roma or San Marzano tomatoes are best for this dip, but any full-flavored tomato can work. In the dead of winter when I crave tomato bruschetta, I use diced organic tomatoes from a can.

Combine the ingredients in a medium bowl shortly before serving at room temperature with the Bruscetta with Olive Oil and Herbs (page 60). For a change, omit the feta and serve the tapenade with slices of fresh goat mozzarella or goat brie.

Christmas Lima Bean Dip

8   **ounces dried Christmas lima beans, soaked overnight**
Garlic oil: 2 cloves garlic, poached in ⅓ cup extra virgin olive oil
½   **teaspoon salt, or to taste**

Look for Christmas lima beans in the dried bean section of your grocery store or go to the Web site www.ranchogordo.com. They are a beautiful deep burgundy color with creamy speckles. Great northerns or cannellini beans make a good substitute. In a pinch, use a can or 2 of rinsed-and-drained beans instead of starting from scratch.

Drain the lima beans and cover with fresh water. Bring to a boil and then simmer for about 30 minutes, or until soft. Reserve ½ cup of the cooking water. Drain and cool.

Place the lima beans in the food processor along with the garlic oil and salt. Pulse until smooth and creamy. If the beans are too stiff, add a little of the cooking water to thin them. Spoon into a serving bowl. You can make this ahead of time but serve at room temperature.

Whole Picnic Ciabatta

1 (1-pound) bag frozen artichoke hearts, partially thawed

1–2 tablespoons olive oil

Salt and pepper to taste

1 tablespoon lemon juice

1 loaf rustic Italian-style bread, like ciabatta or thick focaccia

1 (8-ounce) jar sliced sun-dried tomatoes (the yummy packed in-olive-oil kind)

½ cup pesto (page 47)

3–4 cups cooked and shredded chicken breast

8 ounces semi-hard goat cheese

1 (8-ounce) jar roasted red or yellow peppers

Just about any kind of cheese would taste good on this sandwich. You are limited only by your own imagination. I really like to make this with a manchego-style cheese. Naked Goat would be excellent, as would one of the three-milk cheeses like Ibérico or Montalban. Goat mozzarella would also be a great choice, as would soft chèvre, with which you can never go wrong.

Preheat oven to 425 degrees F. Toss the artichoke hearts in the olive oil, salt and pepper, and roast for about 20 minutes, until they are beginning to brown. Transfer them to a bowl, drizzle with lemon juice and let cool.

Cut the bread in half horizontally to create one huge sandwich. Spread one side thickly with sun-dried tomatoes and the other with pesto. On the tomato side, distribute the chicken and then the artichokes. Cover with cheese slices. Finally, spread peppers on the pesto side. Carefully, pick up the pesto-pepper side and close the sandwich. Press down gently with both hands to encourage the two sides to stick together. At this point, wrap and chill until the sandwich is needed, or slice and serve at room temperature.

Annabel's Purse

4   ounces mixed mushrooms, thinly sliced

¼   white onion, thinly sliced

3   tablespoons unsalted butter

1   teaspoon minced fresh thyme

2   tablespoons Pinot Noir

½   sheet puff pastry, thawed in the fridge

5   ounces goat Brie, chilled in freezer beforehand

1   extra-large free-range egg, beaten

This recipe is from Chef Annabel Rorden, owner of Epiphany Gourmet, who pairs this wonderful appetizer with Pinot Noir. You probably won't have any trouble at all finding goat Brie, as it can be found in all the better grocery stores now, including Trader Joe's. Any variety of mushrooms will do for this recipe, but Annabel suggests shiitake, chanterelles, enoki or portabellas for good flavor.

Preheat oven to 400 degrees F. Sauté mushrooms and onion in butter until the onion is beginning to brown. Add the thyme and the wine, and sauté until the excess liquid has cooked away, about 2 minutes. Let cool.

From the short end of the pastry, cut 3 strips that are the width of the dough and about ⅜ inch thick. On a lightly floured surface, roll the strips between your palm and the board, until they are rounded and have grown about a third longer. Pinch one end of the strips together and then braid them. Twist off the other end to keep from unraveling.

Lightly flour the remaining puff pastry and roll out into an ⅛-inch-thick circle. Place the frozen Brie in the center of the dough and top with the sautéed mushroom mixture, taking care that the vegetables remain on top of the cheese.

Gather the dough around the sides like a purse until you have it pulled together with a slight gap at the center. Pinch together to close the purse and then attach the braid. Drape the edges of the dough down over the braid in places so that it looks like a purse or sack tied at the neck.

Place the purse on a lightly greased baking dish and carefully brush with egg. Bake for 15 minutes; cover with foil at this point to prevent over-browning and bake an additional 10–15 minutes. Let rest for a few minutes before serving with grapes and crusty bread.

Crab and Cheddar Melts with Quick Tomato and Apple Chutney

4 slices sourdough sandwich bread, like Beckman's or Columbus

½ pound Dungeness Crabmeat, picked over for the shells

3 tablespoons mayonnaise

1 teaspoon Dijon mustard

½ cup finely minced scallions

¼ teaspoon Old Bay seasoning

Salt, pepper and Tabasco to taste

6–8 ounces white goat cheddar, sliced

This makes 4 open-faced sandwiches, but you might use sliced baguettes instead and make lots of smaller hors d'oeuvre–size open-faced melts.

Preheat oven to 375 degrees F. Lay the bread slices out on a baking sheet. In a medium bowl, mix the crabmeat with the mayonnaise, mustard, scallions and seasonings. Divide the crab mixture among the bread slices and smooth out. Top with cheddar slices. Bake until the cheese is bubbly and beginning to brown. Serve with the chutney.

Quick Tomato and Apple Chutney

¼ cup extra virgin olive oil

1 medium onion, diced

2 pounds ripe farm-stand tomatoes, diced

2 Granny Smith apples, diced

2 teaspoons brown mustard seeds

¼ teaspoon cayenne

¼ teaspoon allspice

¼ teaspoon cinnamon

½ teaspoon salt

⅓ cup sugar

1 lemon rind, freshly minced

⅓ cup cider vinegar

This chutney is a delicious way to enjoy a bumper crop of tomatoes. Cherry tomatoes, which I usually have an abundance of in late summer, will work as well.

Warm the olive oil in a large deep skillet and add the onion. When the onion is soft, add the tomatoes and apples. Simmer a moment while measuring out the remaining ingredients. Sprinkle the seasonings on the onion mixture, stir and then add the vinegar. Simmer, stirring from time to time for another 20–30 minutes. Serve the chutney warm or at room temperature with the Crab and Cheddar Melts, grilled salmon, grilled cheese sandwiches or scrambled eggs.

Smoked Salmon and Chèvre on Ricotta Dill Bread

4	slices Ricotta Dill Bread (page 24) or dill rye
4	ounces fresh chèvre
4	ounces sliced smoked salmon or lox

Lightly toast the bread if you like it crispy, but let it cool first so you don't melt the chèvre.

Lay bread slices on a work surface. Divide the chèvre and smooth over 2 slices of the bread (stopping just short of the edges if you plan to trim off the crusts). Divide the smoked salmon and arrange it on top of the chèvre. Top with another slice of bread and press down gently. Cut the sandwiches in halves or in quarters and trim the crusts if you like.

Mediterranean Eggplant Wraps

1   medium eggplant, diced
2   red bell peppers, diced
1   medium sweet onion, diced
6–8 garlic cloves, minced
3   tablespoons olive oil
Salt and pepper to taste
4   ounces chèvre
4   (8-inch) soft Mediterranean
    flat breads or flour tortillas
1   cup sliced fresh basil

These are the absolute perfect hors d'oeuvre or picnic food. They can be made and assembled a day in advance and refrigerated. They travel well and will taste even better when they come to room temperature. Wait until the last minute to cut them in halves or, if you like, slice them for little aram-style sandwiches for a party platter.

Preheat oven to 400 degrees F. Combine the eggplant, peppers, onion and garlic in a heavy ovenproof skillet, and toss with the oil, salt and pepper. Roast for about 30–35 minutes, until everything has cooked down and is highly fragrant. Let cool a bit.

ASSEMBLY
Warm the chèvre for 15 seconds on low in a small bowl in the microwave to soften it. Spread ¼ of the warmed chèvre on each flat bread or tortilla. Spoon on some of the eggplant mixture and sprinkle on ¼ cup basil. Roll up from one side, jelly-roll style. At this point, wrap them in plastic wrap and refrigerate until later, if need be. To serve, cut each one in half or slice into appetizer-size pieces.

Soups and Salads

Fresh Spring Pea Soup with Curried Croutons and Minted Fromage Blanc

Hearts of Romaine with Creamy Blue Cheese Dressing

Caprese Salad with Goat Mozzarella

Red Lentil Soup with Peppery Feta Shortbread

Crab, Shrimp and Avocado Salad with Roasted Red Bell Pepper Ranch Dressing

Spinach, Chicken and Orzo Salad with Feta Cheese

Farmstand Lettuce with Baked Goat Cheese Buttons and Rosemary Walnuts

Rustic Carrot and Ginger Soup with Fromage Blanc and Cilantro Pesto

Red Leaf Lettuce, Spiced Pecans and Goat Blue with Honey Blackberry Vinaigrette

Fresh Spring Pea Soup with Curried Croutons and Minted Fromage Blanc

4   cups freshly shelled English
    peas, preferably organic
1   tablespoon butter
1   tablespoon extra virgin olive oil
2   cups diced shallots or Vidalia
    onion
1   quart light chicken stock, pref-
    erably homemade
4   ounces fromage blanc or
    chèvre, or 1 cup yogurt cheese
2   tablespoons freshly minced
    herbs (chives or mint)

CROUTONS
¼   cup extra virgin olive oil
2–3 cloves garlic, minced
1–2 tablespoons curry powder
6–8 slices day-old French or Italian
    bread, sliced or cut in cubes

The season for fresh peas is short, and this soup is an easy way to savor them when they arrive. Shelling the peas takes only 10 or 15 minutes, so don't be intimidated. You will need 4 pounds of peas in the pod. You can shell them in advance and pop them into a ziplock bag where they will wait patiently for you in the fridge for up to a week! If you don't have a goat to feed the empty pods to, put them in the compost bin.

For a quick chicken stock, simply slip a chicken breast with the skin and bones still attached into 6 cups of simmering water. It will take about 15 minutes to cook through. You'll be left with a quart or so of light chicken stock, delicate enough for the sweetness of this soup. Reserve the chicken breast for another use, such as a chicken salad, the Chicken Quesadillas (page 56) or the Whole Picnic Ciabatta (page 67).

Rinse the peas in a colander. In a soup pot, melt the butter with the olive oil. Sauté the shallots or onion until soft. Add the peas and the chicken stock, and bring to a boil. Turn down the heat and simmer until the peas are soft, about 10 minutes. Puree with a hand blender or in batches in a regular blender. In a small bowl, combine the fromage or yogurt cheese and herbs.

CROUTONS
While the peas are still cooking, warm the olive oil in a skillet. Add the garlic and curry powder, and stir. Add the bread cubes or slices and brown on all sides, about 4 or 5 minutes. Serve each bowl of soup with a dollop of herbed fromage or yogurt cheese and a slice or a handful of croutons.

Fresh Yogurt Cheese

To make a cup of yogurt cheese, spoon about a pint of plain goat yogurt into a paper-lined coffee filter cup. Set the filter over a mug to catch the drippings. Let set at room tempera-ture for about 2 hours. You will be left with a thick, tangy yogurt cheese to use any place you might use sour cream or creme fraiche.

Hearts of Romaine with Creamy Blue Cheese Dressing

6–8 ounces mild goat blue cheese

4 ounces buttermilk

1/3 cup mayonnaise

1 clove garlic, blanched for 1 minute in the microwave in 1/4 cup water

2 hearts of romaine, cut in half lengthwise to make 4 wedges

1/4 cup raw or toasted sunflower seeds

Making a creamy dressing is a great way to finish off that hunk of blue cheese left over from your last cheese platter. Just about any goat blue will make a tasty salad dressing. For a mild and creamy goat blue, try Carr Valley Billy Blue from Wisconsin or Lively Run's Cayuga Blue. For something a little more assertive, try Legendairy's chèvre Blue Gouda or Blue de Bocage. If it goes against your nature to mix that expensive cheese in with other ingredients, simply toss your greens in extra virgin olive oil and a good balsamic vinegar, and then crumble those blue beauties over the top.

Place about 2/3 of the blue cheese in the blender with the buttermilk, mayonnaise and the blanched clove of garlic. Add a little of the garlic water only if the dressing is too thick. Pulse until smooth.

Place a wedge of romaine on 4 salad plates. Divide the dressing among the lettuce wedges and sprinkle each with 1 tablespoon of sunflower seeds. Crumble a little of the extra blue cheese over the top.

Caprese Salad with Goat Mozzarella

2 pounds fresh ripe, colorful summer tomatoes, sliced

8 ounces goat mozzarella (farmhouse or Greek Kasseri cheese), sliced

1 bunch fresh basil

Extra virgin olive oil

Balsamic vinegar

Salt and pepper

This salad couldn't be simpler; but, for it to really taste good, you must have REAL tomatoes! Not the hard round, machine-picked things that masquerade as tomatoes in the grocery store. If you don't grow your own, treat yourself to some from your local farmers' market. Sample the different varieties and bring home a couple of pounds of your favorites. Eat them as soon as possible and don't put them in the fridge unless they are in danger of going bad, as you'll ruin the perfect flavor and turn them bitter. Be sure to get some fresh basil while you're there, too!

Use any fresh mild goat cheese that's firm enough to slice. Fraga Farms in Oregon makes organic goat mozzarella and also a farmhouse cheese that's similar in texture to feta but very mild. See Resources on page 136.

Alternately arrange the tomatoes and cheese on a platter or on individual salad plates. Tear leaves from the bunch of basil and tuck them in here and there to create an attractive salad. Drizzle with oil and then with vinegar. Salt and pepper to taste. Eat as soon as possible!

Red Lentil Soup with Peppery Feta Shortbread

4–6 slices applewood smoked bacon
(like Niman Ranch bacon), diced
1 large onion, diced
1–2 tablespoons minced fresh sage
leaves
4 good-size carrots, diced
2 cups petite crimson lentils or
any small red lentils, rinsed
6 cups chicken stock, homemade
(or low-sodium canned is just
fine for this soup)
Peppery Feta Shortbread dough
Salt and freshly ground pepper to
taste

Tiny red lentils from Phipps Ranch in Pescadero make an incredibly delicious soup in just about an hour's time. The aroma of this soup is truly wonderful on a cold winter evening. You can prepare the shortbread dough ahead of time and simply slice and bake while the soup is cooking.

Warm a large, heavy saucepan over medium heat and add the bacon. Cook for 2 minutes and then add the onion. Once the onion is soft, add the sage, carrots, lentils and stock. Bring to a boil and let simmer for about 45 minutes.

Bake the shortbread as directed below. Season the soup with salt and pepper at the table, if needed. The bacon and shortbread may be salty enough, so taste before adding more.

Peppery Feta Shortbread

⅔ cup all-purpose flour
1 tablespoon cornmeal
3 tablespoons butter
3 ounces goat feta
2 tablespoons olive oil
Freshly ground rainbow pepper-
corns

These are nice with the Red Lentil Soup, but they also make a great accompaniment to a glass of full-bodied red wine, as is. A great emergency appetizer for the holidays! Just slice and bake.

Place the flour, cornmeal, butter and feta in the food processor and pulse until crumbly. Add the olive oil and pulse just until the dough begins to hold together. Shape the dough into a little log, like you would for roll cookies. Wrap in plastic wrap and chill for at least an hour or freeze for up to a month. Thaw in the fridge, if time allows. Preheat oven to 375 degrees F. Slice the shortbread and arrange on an ungreased cookie sheet. Grind some pepper over the slices and bake for 8–10 minutes, or until they're just beginning to color around the edges. Serve warm or at room temperature alongside the soup.

Crab, Shrimp and Avocado Salad with Roasted Red Bell Pepper Ranch Dressing

1   large head crisp Romaine lettuce, sliced

2   avocados, halved or sliced

1/2   pound cooked, shelled and chilled crabmeat

1/2   pound cooked bay shrimp, rinsed and chilled

4   hard-boiled eggs, halved or sliced

Cucumber slices, cherry tomato halves and lemon wedges for garnish

Roasted Red Bell Pepper Ranch Dressing, below

1 bunch scallions, diced

As a native San Franciscan, I am compelled to include my favorite seafood salad in this book. I have added fresh goat cheese and roasted red pepper to my favorite ranch dressing, which gives the salad a Louie-style presentation. If you're tempted to use iceberg lettuce to be traditional here, please buy the organic! Otherwise it won't taste like lettuce. Don't forget the sourdough bread!

Divide the lettuce between 4 salad plates. Arrange the avocado halves in the center or fan out the slices. Divide the crab and shrimp and set atop the avocados. Arrange the hard-boiled eggs, cucumber slices, tomatoes and a lemon wedge on each plate. Pour dressing over the top and sprinkle with the scallions.

Roasted Red Bell Pepper Ranch Dressing

1   (5 1/2-ounce) tub Harley Farms fromage blanc or 4 ounces plain chèvre

1/2   cup low-fat buttermilk

1/2   cup light mayonnaise

1   tablespoon fresh lemon juice (about half a small fresh lemon)

1   clove garlic, poached in 1/3 cup water

1   roasted red bell pepper, peeled and diced, divided

1–2 tablespoons, very finely minced shallot, divided

1   tablespoon, finely minced chives

1/2   teaspoon (or more) salt to taste

Freshly ground pepper to taste

Use the leftovers of this ranch dressing as a dip for raw veggies or on our favorite—taco salad!

Place the cheese, buttermilk, mayonnaise and lemon juice in the blender. Blanch the garlic by bringing it to a boil in a small saucepan with the water (or you can do this in the microwave instead if you like). Cool. This will mellow the raw garlic. Add both the garlic and water to the blender. Add half the bell pepper and half the shallot. Blend until smooth. Add the remaining bell pepper, shallot, chives, salt and pepper. Pulse to incorporate the seasonings but don't completely liquefy, as you want a bit of texture.

Pour into a clean pint jar and chill. Keeps for about a week in the fridge. If possible, make the dressing a few hours in advance or the night before. It will thicken nicely in the fridge.

Spinach, Chicken and Orzo Salad with Feta Cheese

2   large boneless, skinless half breasts of chicken (about a pound)

8   ounces orzo pasta

20 pitted Kalamata olives, halved or sliced

1   small red onion, quartered then sliced

1   yellow bell pepper, cut in small strips or squares

1/3 cup extra virgin olive oil

Juice of 2 lemons

1   cup fresh basil leaves, finely chopped

2   cloves garlic, finely chopped

1/3 cup pine nuts

4–5 ounces goat feta

5–6 ounces baby spinach, washed and stemmed

1/2 pint red cherry tomatoes, cut in halves

Salt and pepper to taste

This is a really great salad to take to a picnic or potluck, or just to serve as is for a light supper on a warm night. You can assemble it in advance, tossing in the spinach and tomatoes at the last minute.

Poach the chicken breasts in a pan of salted simmering water for about 10 minutes. When tender, remove from water and put aside to cool. Reserve stock for another use. Meanwhile, cook the orzo about 8 minutes in a large pot of boiling salted water. Using a fine strainer, pour off the water. Rinse in cold water briefly to stop cooking.

In a large salad bowl, toss together the olives, onion, bell pepper, olive oil, lemon juice, basil, garlic and pine nuts, and let sit while dicing the chicken. Add the cooled pasta and the chicken to the salad bowl and crumble the feta between your fingers over the salad and toss again. The salad will hold like this for hours in the fridge; at the last minute add the spinach and the tomatoes. Salt and pepper to taste.

Serve at room temperature for the best flavor.

Farmstand Lettuce with Baked Goat Cheese Buttons and Rosemary Walnuts

Several heads tender young farm-
     stand lettuce or ½ pound baby
     lettuce mix
8   ounces fresh chèvre
2   tablespoons minced herbs, like
      rosemary, thyme and oregano
½   cup extra virgin olive oil, divided
1   clove garlic, sliced
½   cup coarse fresh bread crumbs
2   tablespoons balsamic vinegar
      or lemon juice
1–2 tablespoons Dijon mustard
½   teaspoon honey
Pinch salt
Rosemary Walnuts, below
Fresh baguettes

This salad is dressed in a very simple mustard vinaigrette. I like to flavor the olive oil by first warming it with sliced garlic. Just place a glass measuring cup with the olive oil and garlic into the microwave for 1 minute. Let cool a bit and then discard the garlic. You can bake the goat cheese and the Rosemary Walnuts below, at the same time, if you like.

Preheat oven to 350 degrees F. Wash and dry the lettuce and set aside. Place the chèvre and herbs in a small bowl. Poach the garlic in the oil as directed above. Drizzle 2 tablespoons of the oil onto the chèvre and mix with a fork. Make 4 little chèvre patties and dredge them in the bread crumbs. Set them on a small dish, cover and put into the freezer for about 10–15 minutes.

Pour the remaining oil into the bottom of a large salad bowl. Add the vinegar or lemon juice, mustard, honey and salt. Whisk vigorously until you have a creamy mixture. Gently toss the lettuce in the dressing. Divide among 4 salad plates.

Bake the cheese buttons for about 7 minutes, or until you can detect that the cheese is just beginning to soften. Remove from the oven, cool slightly and then carefully lift with a spatula and place one on top of each salad. Top with some walnuts and serve with slices of fresh or toasted baguettes.

Rosemary Walnuts

1½ cups walnut halves and pieces
1   tablespoon extra virgin olive oil
1   tablespoon fresh or dried rose-
      mary, roughly chopped
Kosher salt

Eat these on their own or use them to garnish a salad or a meatless pasta dish.

Preheat oven to 350 degrees F. In a small baking pan (I use a pie dish) combine the walnuts, olive oil and rosemary. Toss to coat. Spread them out in the pan, sprinkle with a little salt and bake for about 7 or 8 minutes, or until fragrant and beginning to color. Be careful not to burn them as they go from perfect to overdone very quickly!

Rustic Carrot and Ginger Soup with Fromage Blanc and Cilantro Pesto

2   tablespoons butter
2   tablespoons olive oil
1   very large onion, diced
8   cloves garlic, minced
3–4 tablespoon grated fresh ginger
3   pounds organic carrots, cut into
     chunks
¾   teaspoon salt
6   cups chicken or vegetable stock,
     preferably homemade
1   (5.5-ounce) tub Harley Farm
     fromage blanc or some
     crumbled chèvre
Cilantro Pesto (recipe below)

Use organic carrots for this soup if possible. Flavorwise, they are so superior to ordinary store-bought carrots. You can skip peeling them if the skins look nice and "appealing" after they've been scrubbed. When I make this soup, I feed all the carrot tops to the goats.

Melt the butter and oil in a soup pot. Add the onion and cook slowly until soft; then add the garlic and ginger. Stir and cook another minute or so. Add the carrots, salt and stock. Bring to a boil and then turn down and simmer for about 30 minutes. Puree with a hand blender or carefully mash the carrots until the soup is blended but not too smooth. Serve the soup with a dollop of fromage and a drizzle of the pesto.

Cilantro Pesto

1   cup packed cilantro leaves
1   jalapeño, finely minced, and
     seeds discarded
1   clove garlic
¼   cup toasted pumpkin seeds
     (toast 5 minutes at 325
     degrees F)
2   tablespoons or so olive oil
¼   teaspoon salt

Use cilantro pesto drizzled on the carrot and ginger soup or spoon it on freshly grilled salmon with a side of the Crispy Cumin-and-Ginger Potatoes (page 41).

Place the cilantro, jalapeño, garlic, pumpkin seeds, olive oil and salt into the food processor or mini-chop and pulse until combined.

Red Leaf Lettuce, Spiced Pecans and Goat Blue with Honey Blackberry Vinaigrette

1   good-size head red leaf lettuce, or 2 small heads of red butter lettuce
1   handful blackberries, divided
2   tablespoons good-quality balsamic vinegar
1   tablespoon honey
4   tablespoons extra virgin olive oil
Salt and pepper to taste
4–6 scallions, chopped, or some sliced red onion
1   cup or more Spiced Pecans (recipe below)
4–6 ounces Billy Blue (or any crumbly goat blue you can find)

Discovering goat blue recently was such an unexpected event. I didn't even know it existed! Carr Valley Billy Blue, a mild goat blue from Wisconsin, was my first brush with this, but since then, I have found others. Many of them are imports, like the wonderful Bleu de Bocage by Pascal Beillevaire from the Loire Valley or the Legendairy Blue Chèvre from Holland. There are some true blue home boys as well. Look for Chèvre in Blue by Montchèvre, Rouge et Noir's Marin Chèvre Blue, Lively Run's Cayuga Blue from New York State and others. Add sliced chicken breast for a delightful main course salad.

Wash, spin-dry and tear lettuce into bite-size pieces. Set aside.

Mash a few berries in the bottom of a small bowl with a fork. Add the vinegar and the honey. Warm slightly in the microwave to melt the honey. Whisk in the oil, salt and pepper. Pour over the lettuce and toss.

Divide the lettuce among 4 salad plates. Sprinkle each serving with some onions, pecans and a few berries and, finally, crumble the blue cheese over the top and serve.

Spiced Pecans

¼   cup mesquite honey
2   cups pecan halves
¼   cup raw sugar
½   teaspoon ground cumin
¼   teaspoon salt
¼   teaspoon cinnamon
Pinch cayenne pepper

These pecans are great on a savory salad like the one above or on a spinach salad, but they also make a wonderful topping on ice cream or over a fresh fruit salad at breakfast.

Preheat oven to 350 degrees F. Cover a small baking sheet with parchment. In a medium bowl, warm the mesquite honey in the microwave for 15 seconds. Add pecan halves and toss to coat.

Combine sugar, ground cumin, salt, cinnamon and cayenne. Toss with the nuts, spread out on the baking sheet and bake for about 10 minutes. Let cool a bit before handling or nibbling!

Main Dishes and Pastas

Artichoke and Chicken Cannelloni

Buffalo Feta Burgers with Sweet Potato Fries

Saffron Fettuccine Carbonara with Roasted Asparagus

Butternut, Portabella and Chicken Italian Sausage Lasagne

Eggplant, Red Bell Pepper and Pesto Lasagne

Golden Zucchini Gratin with Feta, Tomatoes and Pine Nuts

Grilled Lamb Tenderloins Stuffed with Eggplant and Feta

Sweet Potato Gnocchi with Tomatoes, Walnuts and Sage

Wild Salmon Tacos with Roasted Corn and Chile Adobo Cream

Crispy Pork or Chicken Cutlets with Garlic-and-Rosemary Mashed Potatoes

Kid's Mac 'n' Cheese

Artichoke and Chicken Cannelloni

10–12 ounces fresh pasta sheets, cut into 4 x 6-inch squares or to fit your baking pan, or boxed flat-dried lasagne sheets

1 large onion, chopped

2–3 tablespoons olive oil

8 cloves garlic, minced

¼ cup freshly minced herbs, like thyme, oregano and/or parsley

1 (15-ounce) can artichoke hearts, quartered or roughly chopped

2½–3 cups diced or shredded cooked chicken breast

1 (15-ounce) can organic diced tomatoes, drained

BÉCHAMEL AND CHEESE TOPPING

2 tablespoons butter

2 tablespoons flour

2 cups whole goat milk

2 cups grated goat Gouda

If you can find fresh pasta sheets by the pound, you can customize the size of the cannelloni to your favorite baking dish. They will swell when boiled, so cut the squares a bit smaller than the width of the pan.

Preheat oven to 350 degrees F. Put on a large pot of salted water to boil for the pasta.

Sauté the onion in the olive oil until softened. Add the garlic and herbs, and cook for another minute. Add the artichokes and chicken. When fully hot, add the tomatoes. Keep on low until ready to use.

Partially cook the pasta now—2 minutes for the fresh pasta, about 4 minutes for the dried. It should be limp but not fully cooked. Drain and stretch the sheets out carefully on a plate. On a separate plate, take one sheet, spread some fill-ing along one long edge and roll. Arrange seam side down in an oiled baking dish. Repeat until your pan is fully packed.

BÉCHAMEL AND CHEESE TOPPING

Melt the butter in a small saucepan. Whisk in the flour and cook for 2 minutes. Gradually add the milk, whisking constantly until smooth. Let the sauce cook, whisking often for several minutes until it begins to thicken. Pour over the cannelloni and sprinkle on the grated cheese. Bake uncovered for about 35 minutes until the cheese is melted and bubbly, and the top is just beginning to brown. Let cool for 5–10 minutes and serve.

Buffalo Feta Burgers with Sweet Potato Fries

1¼ pounds ground buffalo

4 ounces goat feta

¼ cup finely minced shallot

Freshly ground pepper

2–3 tablespoons olive oil

2 tablespoons fresh thyme
   leaves

Pinch salt

4 lightly toasted buns

Thick slices of tomato

Lettuce leaves

Spicy mustard (your favorite)

Although I am not a big red-meat eater, I do occasionally cave in and bring home some ground buffalo. It's very, very lean, so be careful not to overcook it. The feta and shallots help keep the burgers juicy and add to the really special flavor of the meat. The sweet potato fries add a nice contrast and are so easy to make.

Combine the buffalo, feta, shallot and pepper in a bowl with your hands. Form 4 burgers and set on a plate. Combine the olive oil, thyme and salt in a small bowl. Warm for 15 seconds in the microwave. Heat stove top, charcoal or gas grill (or cook them in a heavy skillet, if you prefer) and proceed as you would for beef burgers. Baste the burgers with oil on both sides as they cook. Cook about 5–6 minutes a side for medium. Let the burgers rest for 5 minutes while you toast the buns. Top with tomato and lettuce, and serve with a side of Sweet Potato Fries. Pass the mustard.

Sweet Potato Fries

2 medium-large Garnet sweet
   potatoes, peeled and cut into
   wedges

2 tablespoons olive oil

Kosher salt to taste

Use any variety of sweet potato you like, but I prefer to use organic garnet yams for their deep rich color. Kids love these fries!

Preheat oven to 400 degrees F. Toss the sweet potatoes and olive oil together in a bowl to coat. Spread out on a cookie sheet, sprinkle with salt and bake for about 20–25 minutes, until lightly brown and slightly crisp.

Saffron Fettuccine Carbonara with Roasted Asparagus

1   teaspoon salt
8   ounces dried saffron fettuc-
     cine
6   slices natural applewood
     smoked bacon, like Niman
     Ranch's
2   tablespoons extra virgin olive
     oil
1   very large onion, halved and
     then sliced
1   cup chicken stock or pasta
     water
2   egg yolks
½   cup (or more to taste) very
     finely grated hard goat
     cheese*

This is hands down my son's favorite pasta dinner. The flavor of the bacon and the onions to-gether is what makes this simple dish so good.

Put a large pot of water on to boil. Place soup or pasta plates in a warm oven. Once the water has come to a full boil, add salt and fettuccine. Set the timer for the pasta (the package will tell you how long, and subtract a minute) and start the sauce.

Dice the bacon and place in a deep skillet, large enough for both the sauce and the pasta. Cook the bacon until it's just beginning to brown; drain off most of the fat. Add the olive oil to the pan in place of the bacon fat. Add the onion and cook until soft and beginning to brown, about 10 minutes. While the onion is cooking, drain the lin-guine. Add the stock or water to the pan of onion and let simmer a moment or two before adding the drained pasta, tossing to mix. Once the pasta and onion mixture is piping hot, remove from the heat and add one egg yolk at a time, continuing to toss to coat the pasta. Finally add the grated cheese, toss and then serve immediately in your warmed bowls or plates. Pass the pepper grinder at the table.

CHEESE SUGGESTIONS*

Achadinha's aged Capricious, Cypress Grove's Midnight Moon aged goat Gouda, Capra Sarda, Cabralinda or any hard goat cheese with the texture of Parmigiano Reggiano or Pecorino Romano.

Roasted Asparagus

1   pound trimmed asparagus
     spears
1   tablespoon extra virgin olive
     oil
1   tablespoon good-quality
     balsamic vinegar
Salt
Freshly ground pepper

This makes an easy and delicious side dish. It's great with the Saffron Fettuccine, above, or alongside grilled salmon or chicken. You can even grill the asparagus instead of roasting it!

This makes a wonderful side for this dish. Toss asparagus with olive oil and balsamic vinegar. Spread on a baking sheet, season with salt and pepper, and roast at 400 degrees F for about 12–15 minutes while you prepare the pasta.

Butternut, Portabella and Chicken Italian Sausage Lasagne

1 **small butternut squash, diced small (about 3–4 cups)**

2 **red bell peppers, quartered and then sliced**

1 **small red onion, chopped**

6 **cloves garlic, minced**

1–2 **tablespoons olive oil**

Salt and pepper to taste

12 **ounces fresh lasagne or pasta sheets**

1 **pound goat ricotta, or 8 ounces ricotta mixed with 8 ounces chèvre**

2 **eggs**

Grated nutmeg

4 **chicken Italian sausages, about 1 pound total (I like using 2 spicy hot and 2 mild)**

1 **tablespoon olive oil**

3–4 **cups marinara sauce, preferably homemade**

12 **ounces shredded goat Gouda or mozzarella**

8 **ounces portabella mushrooms, sliced**

This lasagne can be made using any variety of winter squash, but I really like the butternut squash's slightly sweet flavor in contrast to that of the earthy mushrooms and spicy sausage. Roasting the cubes of squash really brings out the best flavor.

Preheat oven to 400 degrees F. Combine the butternut squash, red bell peppers, onion, garlic, olive oil, salt and pepper in an ovenproof dish or skillet. Roast until nicely browned, about 25–30 minutes. Stir once halfway through the cooking.

Meanwhile, bring a large pot of salted water to a boil. Partially cook the lasagne for 2–3 minutes. Drain and carefully lay them out onto a plate until ready to assemble the layers.

Combine the ricotta, eggs and a few gratings of nutmeg in a bowl. A standing mixer works well for this but isn't necessary. If doing by hand, you can soften the ricotta by warming it in the microwave for about a minute. Set aside.

Cut open the sausages, remove the skin and crumble the meat into a medium hot skillet with the other tablespoon of olive oil, and brown.

To assemble the lasagne, start with an oiled 10 x 15-inch baking dish. I like glass because you can see the cooking progress. Spread ½ cup marinara sauce over the bottom evenly. Then layer ⅓ of the pasta sheets (about 4), the ricotta mixture, another third of the noodles, the browned sausage meat, the roasted butternut mixture and the last third of pasta. Top with the rest of the marinara and then the grated cheese. Finally, arrange the sliced mushrooms over the top. Cover with foil.

Bake covered at 350 degrees F for 45 minutes and then uncovered 15 minutes more. Let rest 10–15 minutes before cutting.

BAKING SUGGESTION

You may prepare this dish entirely in advance and bake later or the following day. If you do this, add 10–15 minutes to the covered baking time to make up for the cold interior.

Eggplant, Red Bell Pepper and Pesto Lasagne

1	medium eggplant, quartered and sliced
2	large red bell peppers, sliced
1	medium red onion, chopped
8	cloves garlic, minced
2	tablespoons olive oil
12	ounces fresh pasta sheets
8	ounces goat ricotta
8	ounces chèvre
1	extra-large free-range egg
3–4	cups good marinara sauce, preferably homemade
1	pound smallish zucchini, sliced lengthwise
1	cup pesto, homemade or store bought
12	ounces sliced or grated cheese for the top, preferably goat mozzarella

If I were sent to another planet and could only take one goat cheese recipe along, this would be it! I wonder if someday UPS will ship mozzarella to outer space! Special packaging?

Preheat oven to 425 degrees F. Toss the eggplant, bell peppers, onion and garlic in the olive oil in an ovenproof dish. Roast in the oven for about 25 minutes, stirring once about halfway through. Remove and cool. Turn oven down to 350 degrees F.

While the eggplant is roasting, bring a large pot of salted water to a boil. Partially cook the pasta sheets, about 2–3 minutes, drain and lay out on a plate until ready to use.

Combine the ricotta, chèvre and egg in a mixing bowl. Set aside.

Begin with a baking dish 9 x 12 or 10 x 15 inches. Spread about a cup of marinara sauce on the bottom. Place a third of the lasagne sheets on the sauce. Spread all the chèvre-ricotta mixture evenly over them and top with the slices of zucchini. Layer another third of the pasta sheets. Spread the pesto over them and then the eggplant mixture. Finally, layer the last third of the pasta, the remainder of the sauce and then the sliced or grated cheese over the top.

Cover with foil and bake for about 45 minutes, then remove the foil and bake for another 15 minutes to finish the top. Let rest for 10 minutes before cutting.

(This dish can be prepared a day in advance and refrigerated unbaked. Be sure to add a good 10 or 15 minutes to the cooking time, as the lasagne will be very cold inside.)

Golden Zucchini Gratin with Feta, Tomatoes and Pine Nuts

¹/₃ cup extra virgin olive oil, for sautéing, divided

4–5 slices of day-old French or Italian bread, cut into cubes

1¹/₂–2 pounds golden zucchini or sunburst squash, sliced

1 large torpedo onion, quartered and sliced

1 handful mixed fresh herbs (such as thyme, oregano, Italian parsley), minced

5–6 cloves garlic, minced

Salt and pepper to taste

2–3 extra-large free-range eggs, beaten

4–6 ounces goat feta

2–3 plum tomatoes, chopped

Handful pine nuts

When we have company for dinner, I make this as a side dish for roasted or grilled chicken; but when I make it for my family, it's always the main course!

Preheat oven to 375 degrees F. Place 2–3 tablespoons of olive oil in a hot skillet. Toss in the bread cubes. Brown slightly all around and transfer them to an oiled gratin dish, about 7 x 11 inches, or a very large deep pie dish, spreading them evenly over the bottom.

Wipe the frying pan with a paper towel. Add another 2 tablespoons or so of olive oil and when hot, add the slices of zucchini. Sauté over a medium-high flame to color them, but don't let them cook thoroughly. Transfer them to a bowl and set aside. Add 1 more tablespoon of olive oil to the pan and sauté the onion, letting them soften and brown slightly. Finally, add the herbs and minced garlic and cook 1 more minute. Stir

the squash back into the pan. Salt and pepper if you like, but remember the feta will be a bit salty. Push the squash mixture towards the sides of the pan and add the beaten eggs to the center, turn off the flame and stir to mix with other ingredients. Once the egg is nicely distributed and holding things together, transfer this into the gratin dish and spread it atop the bread cubes.

Crumble the feta over the zucchini. Sprinkle the tomatoes and pine nuts on the top. Add some fresh pepper if you wish and cover with foil. Bake covered 20–25 minutes and then uncovered another 15 minutes to brown the top a little. Let it sit for 10 minutes before serving.

Grilled Lamb Tenderloins Stuffed with Eggplant and Feta

2   (1-pound) boneless lamb
    tenderloins
2   tablespoons Epiphany Mid
    East-West spice rub or your
    favorite lamb/chicken rub
2   Japanese eggplants, sliced
    1/3 inch thick lengthwise
    (you'll need 6 slices, 3 for
    each roll)

FILLING
1   tablespoon olive oil, plus
    some for brushing
1   small red onion, diced
6–8 cloves garlic
4–6 ounces goat feta
1/3 cup golden raisins
1/3 cup pine nuts
Freshly ground pepper
Kitchen string

Any lamb or chicken rub will work for this dish, but if you get a chance, try the Epiphany Mid East-West Blend. It uses "an exotic blend of Persian spices with a Western flare." Somehow it's exactly right for this combination.

Prepare your charcoal, gas or stove-top grill.

Pound the tenderloins to an even 1/2 inch thickness. Sprinkle the lamb with the spice rub and let it sit while preparing the other ingredients. Brush the eggplant slices with a little oil and grill until nicely browned on both sides.

FILLING
Sauté the onion in oil for about 2 minutes. Add garlic and cook a minute longer. Cool slightly. In a small bowl, combine the onion and garlic, feta, raisins, pine nuts and some freshly ground pepper.

ASSEMBLY
Place several slices of eggplant on top of each of the tenderloins, spread half the feta mixture and fold over. Tie up with kitchen string like a miniature roast to keep the filling contained.

Carefully, place on the hot grill. Cook approximately 10–12 minutes per side until medium rare/medium. (If you chilled them after assembling, be sure to add a couple of extra minutes to the cooking time.) Let them rest a few minutes, covered tightly in foil, while preparing to serve dinner.

When everything else is ready, cut each roll in thirds or slices, remove the string and serve immediately.

Sweet Potato Gnocchi with Tomatoes, Walnuts and Sage

1   pound goat ricotta

1½ pounds fresh Garnet sweet
      potatoes, baked or micro-
      waved in the skin until soft

½   cup all-purpose flour, plus ½
      cup for dusting

2   extra-large free-range eggs

1   teaspoon sea salt

Freshly ground pepper

Freshly ground nutmeg

4   tablespoons extra virgin olive
      oil or butter

6   fresh sage leaves, sliced

4   cloves garlic, minced, or 1
      small red onion, chopped

1   cup toasted walnuts

1   pound farm-stand meaty
      tomatoes, sliced

Freshly grated Capra Sarda or
      other hard grating cheese

If you've ever mixed cookie dough, you are over-qualified to make these easy little gems. Mix 'em, roll 'em, chill 'em and drop 'em into boiling water for a few short minutes and then into a simple sauté of tomatoes and herbs. You can order the ricotta online and keep it in the freezer until you are ready to make these.

Crumble the ricotta into a large mixing bowl. Cut open the warm sweet potatoes and scoop the insides into the bowl with the ricotta. Discard the skins. Using a fork, mix the cheese and sweet potato until smooth. Add ½ cup of flour and the eggs, salt, pepper and nutmeg. Mix thoroughly.

Sprinkle 1–2 tablespoons of the remaining flour on a platter. Pour the rest of the flour into a shallow bowl. Spoon the dough by teaspoonfuls and drop into the bowl of flour, a few at a time, dredging them and then rolling them between your palms. Place the floured balls onto the floured platter, cover with plastic wrap and chill for at least an hour or up to 24 hours until ready to cook.

Put on a large pot of water to boil. Add a teaspoon of salt, if desired. Prepare the sauce while waiting for the water to boil.

Warm a large skillet and add the olive oil. Then add sage and garlic or onion. After a minute, add the walnuts. Gently add the sliced tomatoes and sauté for about 5 minutes. Remove from heat and wait for the gnocchi.

Drop the gnocchi in the boiling water. Very gently stir once; after 3–4 minutes, they will begin to float to the surface. Taste one to be sure it's not gummy. As they float to the surface, remove them to a colander one by one. Gently rotate the colander to get rid of any excess water and then slide the gnocchi into the pan with the tomatoes; turn the heat to medium and coat gnocchi with the sauce. Let them sit for a few minutes in the sauce and then serve immediately. Pass the grated cheese at the table.

Wild Salmon Tacos with Roasted Corn and Chile Adobo Cream

3   cups corn kernels, cut fresh
    from the cob or frozen

1/2   red onion, diced

1   red or orange bell pepper,
    diced

2   tablespoons olive oil, divided

Salt and pepper to taste

1 1/2   pounds wild salmon fillet

8   small flour tortillas

GARNISH

Sliced avocado, cucumber, and
    cherry tomatoes

I never get tired of having salmon for dinner. Sometimes we serve these soft tacos when we want a really informal company meal. Roast the corn kernels alone or with red bell pepper and onions, and add cooked baby green limas for a quick succotash-style corn.

Heat a charcoal, gas or stove top grill for the salmon.

Preheat oven to 400 degrees F for the corn. Toss the corn, onion and bell pepper in 1 tablespoon of the olive oil. Season with salt and pepper. Roast in an ovenproof dish for 20–25 minutes until the corn is lightly brown and fragrant.

While the corn is roasting, brush the salmon with the remaining olive oil and place on the hot grill, about 5 minutes per side. Once the salmon is off the grill, let it rest a few minutes, keeping it warm, wrapped in foil until you are ready to assemble the tacos.

Warm the tortillas briefly on the grill. Wrap in a kitchen towel to keep warm.

Place everything on the table and let everyone assemble their own tacos, passing the Chile Adobo Cream.

Chile Adobo Cream

4   ounces chèvre or fromage
    blanc

1/2   cup buttermilk

2–3   tablespoons canned chipotle
    chiles in adobo sauce

You can adjust the heat on this sauce by adding a little more or a little less of the chiles.

Whisk together the chèvre or fromage, buttermilk and chipotles in a bowl or in the blender. Pour into a small serving dish.

Crispy Pork or Chicken Cutlets with Garlic-and-Rosemary Mashed Potatoes

1   pound pork tenderloin or bone-less skinless chicken breasts

½   cup flour

1   extra-large free-range egg, beaten

1   cup fresh bread crumbs, made from day-old French bread

½   cup finely grated aged goat cheese

Olive oil for frying

Salt and pepper to taste

Any well-aged cheese that will grate finely can work for this recipe. Try asking at the cheese counter for Cabralinda from Nicalau Farms or Capra Sarda. A well-aged piece of Achadinhea's Capricious or Bodega Shepherd would be great as well.

Preheat oven to 325 degrees F. Using a sharp knife, butterfly the meat if thick. Spread the meat out flat on a large wooden cutting board or worktable. Cover with plastic wrap and pound until relatively even in thickness, about 1/3 inch thick. Cut into 8 or 9 smaller pieces.

Set out 3 shallow dishes. Put the flour in the first and the egg in the second, and combine the bread crumbs and grated cheese in the third. Dredge each cutlet first in flour, then in egg and lastly in the bread-crumb mixture. Set them on a large plate. At this point, you may cover and refrigerate the breaded cutlets for up to 2 hours.

Warm a large skillet over medium heat and add olive oil about ¼ inch deep. Add the cutlets and cook about 3–4 minutes per side, or until nicely browned. If necessary, reduce heat to prevent the cutlets from browning too fast and getting tough. Once they are nicely browned on both sides, remove to a warm platter.

Garlic-and-Rosemary Mashed Potatoes

2   pounds organic Yukon golds, peeled if desired and cut into chunks

1   teaspoon salt

6–8 cloves garlic, peeled

⅓   cup extra virgin olive oil

4–5 sprigs fresh rosemary (use the tender tips only, stems removed)

3   ounces fromage, blanc or plain goat yogurt

Cover the potato chunks with fresh water, add the salt and bring to a boil. Reduce the heat and simmer for 15 minutes.

Meanwhile, simmer the peeled garlic in the olive oil in a small saucepan for 3–4 minutes. Add the rosemary and remove from the heat. The garlic will continue to cook for a few minutes longer and take on a lovely brown color.

Pierce the potatoes to make sure they are nice and soft. Drain the water and return them to the pan. Take a few serving spoonfuls of the potatoes and combine them with the olive oil mixture in the food processor or mini chop, or you may prefer to just mash them by hand to incorporate the garlic. Once smooth, return to the pot with the rest of the potatoes and mash, adding the fromage or yogurt and salt and pepper to taste. Don't worry about a few lumps. They improve the texture. Serve immediately.

Kid's Mac 'n' Cheese

2¹/₂ cups warm milk (goat milk if
    you have it!)
1   extra-large free-range egg
1   pinch paprika or cayenne
¹/₈ teaspoon nutmeg
1–2 tablespoons achiote oil (op-
    tional, page 64)
12–16 ounces grated goat cheddar
1   pound elbow macaroni, or any
    shape you like
Fresh bread crumbs, tossed in a
    little melted butter or olive oil

Little blue boxes of instant macaroni and cheese are just fine for the emergency supply kit but not very good for feeding your little ones regularly. With only 15 minutes of working time, you can serve up a fresh and scrumptious Mac 'n' Cheese that's loaded with protein and calcium. If you want that nice orange hue, add a tablespoon or 2 of achiote oil, which is simply oil that's been warmed with natural annatto seeds (the orange seed used to color cheddar cheese), or just add a couple of handfuls of finely grated carrots.

Preheat oven to 350 degrees F. Then bring a large pot of salted water to a boil.

Oil a 7 x 11-inch baking dish. Warm the milk in a saucepan on low. Once it's warm to the touch, turn off the heat and whisk in the egg, cayenne and nutmeg. Add the achiote oil, if using.

Cook the pasta, removing it from the water about 2 minutes short of the recommended cooking time so that it's still pretty toothy. Drain in a colander.

In the baking dish, layer half the pasta and half the cheese. Repeat. After one final whisk of the milk mixture, pour it over the pasta. Cover with foil and bake for about 25–30 minutes. Uncover, sprinkle with the bread crumbs and bake for 10

additional minutes to brown the top. For neater portions, let cool a few minutes before serving.

BAKING SUGGESTION
Double this recipe for loads of leftovers, using a 9 x 12 inch or a 10 x 15-inch baking dish. You may need to increase the baking time a few minutes. It's done when it looks slightly brown on top and doesn't jiggle when you move the pan.

CHEESE SUGGESTION
Any goat cheddar will work here, especially one that is slightly aged. Try Harvest Hillman, Achadinhea's Capricious or an aged goat Gouda for a slightly more "grown-up" cheese flavor.

Desserts

Cherry Almond Tart

Espresso Cheesecake Brownies

French Vanilla Gelato

Red Plum Sorbet

Mag's Irish Coffee with Sweet Fromage Blanc Whipped Cream

Three-Layer Chocolate Cake with Sweet Fromage Blanc Whipped Cream

Peanut Butter Mudd Pie with Espresso Caramel Sauce

Bananny Cake with Cream Cheese Icing

Bartlett Pear Tart with Honey and Fromage Blanc

Cherry Almond Tart

TOPPING

2	tablespoons unsalted butter
1	pound dark pitted cherries, fresh or frozen
3/4	cup brown sugar

CRUST

1 1/3	cups all-purpose flour
1/2	cup almonds, toasted and then ground into coarse flour
1/4	cup sugar
1/4	teaspoon salt
6	tablespoons cold unsalted butter
1	extra-large free-range egg

FILLING

8	ounces goat Ricotta
8–10	ounces fromage blanc or chèvre
2/3	cup sugar
2	extra-large free-range eggs
Juice and zest of 1 lemon	

Use fresh cherries if it's cherry season. Otherwise, use frozen pitted organic dark cherries or try blueberries instead.

TOPPING

Start by making the topping so it can cool. Melt the butter in a large ovenproof skillet or saucepan. Add the cherries and stir to coat them in the butter. Sprinkle the sugar over them and continue to stir. Bring to a full rolling boil (or roast in the oven), letting the liquid boil off so that you are left with a nice thick cherry topping. Set aside to cool.

CRUST

Lightly oil a 9- or 10-inch springform pan. Preheat oven to 350 degrees F. Place the flour, almonds, sugar and salt in a large bowl or in the food processor, if you prefer. Mix thoroughly. Slice the butter into the bowl and blend, using a hand pastry blender (or pulsing if using the food processor) until the mixture resembles coarse cornmeal. Add the egg and blend with a fork (or pulse gently in the food processor). Don't be tempted to add any water at this point. Just be patient and continue to mix with the fork. Eventually, the dough takes on a very soft, almost oily feel from the almonds and becomes easy to work. Knead the dough with floured hands on a lightly floured surface. Roll or press into a round the size of the bottom of your pan. Press neatly into place in the pan. Freeze for 15 minutes while you preheat oven and then prebake the shell on a cookie sheet for about 12 minutes.

FILLING

In the bowl of a standing mixer or in the same bowl used to mix the dough, combine the filling ingredients, blending until smooth. Pour over the warm crust and bake until puffy and slightly cracking around the edges, 40–45 minutes. Remove from oven and spoon the cherries over the top. Return the cake to the oven for 5 minutes and then cool on a rack. When completely cooled, chill in springform pan until ready to serve.

Espresso Cheesecake Brownies

7 ounces 70 percent bittersweet chocolate, broken into chunks

1 (1-ounce) square unsweetened chocolate

6 tablespoons unsalted butter

1/4 teaspoon salt

3/4 cup sugar

2 extra-large free-range eggs

1/2 cup all-purpose flour

1 cup pecan halves

TOPPING

4 ounces fromage blanc or fresh chèvre

1/4 cup shot of freshly made espresso or very, very strong fresh drip coffee, cooled

3 tablespoons powdered sugar

1/2 teaspoon vanilla

1/2 beaten egg (about 2 table-spoons)

This is what happens when Scharffenberger chocolate and Peet's coffee meet Harley Farms goat cheese! How can you go wrong? Double this recipe for a larger batch and use a 9 x 12-inch pan. Be prepared to become very popular!

Preheat oven to 325 degrees F. Line an 8 x 8-inch baking pan with parchment that is oiled or buttered on both sides.

Melt the chocolates with the butter over simmering water in a double boiler; or do it my way—on the defrost setting in the microwave—until the chocolates are just about melted. Remove from heat and whisk in the salt and sugar. Add the eggs one at a time. Add the flour and mix thoroughly. The batter should be satiny and dark and pulling away from the sides of the bowl. Scatter the nuts on the bottom of the prepared pan. Spoon all but 1/2 cup of the chocolate mixture into the pan.

TOPPING

Whisk together the fromage, cooled espresso, powdered sugar, vanilla and egg. Drizzle the fromage mixture over the chocolate batter. Dot the remaining chocolate batter over the top of that and run a knife back and forth through the batter to create kind of a swirl pattern over the top.

Bake at 325 degrees F for 30–35 minutes, or until the top is set but not dry. Cool on a rack. Chill thoroughly before cutting if you want nice neat pieces, but be sure to take the brownies out of the fridge a little while before eating. The flavor is so much better when they are at room temp!

French Vanilla Gelato

3   cups goat milk, divided

¾   cup sugar

1   vanilla bean

4   egg yolks

6–8 ounces fromage blanc or very fresh plain chèvre, well chilled

If Ben and Jerry made goat's milk gelato, this is what it would taste like! Serve this on its own, in a sundae or on top of the Espresso Cheesecake Brownies (page 114) or apple pie! Be sure to put your ice cream freezer bowl in the freezer overnight and allow some time to chill the batter before using.

Chill the ice cream freezer bowl overnight.

In a medium saucepan on low, begin warming 2 cups of the milk. Whisk in the sugar. With a sharp knife, cut the vanilla bean in half lengthwise and scrape the seeds into the milk. Add the pod as well and bring the mixture to scalding. Be careful not to let it boil. Set it aside to cool a bit.

In a large bowl, whisk the yolks and the remaining milk until pale, about 2 minutes. Slowly pour the hot milk mixture into the egg mixture, whisking together while pouring. Pour it all back into the saucepan now and heat slowly for about 5 minutes or so. Do not allow it to boil. Cool for a few minutes and then pour it through a fine strainer into the carafe of the blender, discarding the vanilla pods. Refrigerate for several hours or overnight.

When ready to make the gelato, add the fromage blanc to the blender and combine. Remove the ice cream bowl from the freezer, set it in place and immediately pour in the chilled gelato mixture, following the instructions for your machine. It will take about 30 minutes for the gelato to freeze. You can eat it right away or spoon the gelato into a freezer container and place immediately into the freezer until ready to eat. Freezing the gelato for an hour or more before serving improves the scooping consistency.

SUNDAE SUGGESTION

For an extra-special treat, try smothering the vanilla gelato in the Espresso Caramel Sauce (page 122) and then sprinkling on some Spiced Pecans (page 90), or put a scoop into a tall chilled glass of old fashioned root beer and feel like a kid again.

Red Plum Sorbet

2 cups water

1³/₄ cups sugar

1¹/₂ pounds tree-ripened red plums, pitted and chunked (about 3 cups)

4 ounces fromage blanc

Our property luckily came with a plum tree. If you have a neighbor with a plum tree, it's best to make friends. Life is short, but then so is the plum season!

Make the simple syrup by combining the water and sugar in a small saucepan and bringing it to a boil. Chill for several hours or overnight.

Pit the plums and cut into chunks. Scrape the juice and chunks into the blender, add the fromage blanc and pulse to blend. Don't over process. You want a few chunks for texture.

Remove the ice cream bowl from the freezer and attach to the machine. Proceed with the manufacturer's instructions. It should take about 30 minutes to freeze. You can eat the sorbet right away or, for better texture and nice clean scoops, freeze in a quart container for a couple of hours.

Mag's Irish Coffee with Sweet Fromage Blanc Whipped Cream

1 (4-ounce) cup strong coffee (regular or decaf) or double shot of espresso

1 (1¹/₂- to 2-ounce) shot Irish whiskey, Jack Daniels or Maker's Mark

1 dollop of Sweet Fromage Blanc Whipped Cream (page 120)

Grated bittersweet chocolate

Cinnamon sticks, to use as swizzle sticks

If you don't have an espresso machine, no problem. Simply make some very strong drip coffee instead. Peet's Holiday Blend and a bar of Scharffenberger 70 percent bittersweet would be just the thing for these. Add gingerbread and you'll be sure to hear reindeer on the roof!

Pour coffee or espresso into a festive heat-proof glass mug appropriate for the size of a cup of coffee. Add the whiskey and a dollop of Sweet Fromage Blanc Whipped Cream. Decorate with some grated chocolate and slip in a cinnamon stick. Serve immediately.

Three-Layer Chocolate Cake with Sweet Fromage Blanc Whipped Cream

3   cups all-purpose flour
2   cups sugar
1/2 cup cocoa powder (I add an extra couple of tablespoons)
2   teaspoons baking soda
1   teaspoon salt
2/3 cup canola oil
2   tablespoons white vinegar
1   teaspoon vanilla
2   cups cold water

Any chocolate layer cake will go nicely with this rich whipped cream, but I like this particular cake, as it is so light that it really showcases the fromage cream. The unusual thing about this batter is that it contains no eggs or butter, yet it has a wonderful taste and texture. Turns out this recipe dates back to the Depression when bakers had to make do to get around the lack of butter and eggs at the time. I hadn't made this cake in years, but it resurfaced recently when my friend Sue Lagow made it for my birthday. She baked it in three layers, and we covered it in this Sweet Fromage Blanc Whipped Cream—it was birthday heaven! I like to think of it as my Anti-Depression Cake!

Preheat oven to 350 degrees F. Coat three 9 x 2-inch round cake pans with cooking spray and then line the bottoms with rounds of parchment paper. Lightly mist the parchment and then coat the pans lightly with flour. Don't skip this step or the cake will stick!

Combine the dry ingredients in a large bowl. Stir the wet ingredients together in a separate bowl and then add to the dry ingredients, beating for 1 minute to combine. Divide the batter between the prepared pans and bake for 30–35 minutes, until the cake springs back when touched.

Cool on a rack for 10–15 minutes. Remove from the pans to cool completely before frosting with Sweet Fromage Blanc Whipped Cream. Add fresh berries for a finishing touch.

Sweet Fromage Blanc Whipped Cream

1   pint whipping cream
1   (5 1/2-ounce) tub Harley Farms Fromage Blanc
3–4 tablespoons sugar or honey, or to taste
1   teaspoon vanilla

Adding fromage blanc to ordinary whipped cream somehow rounds out the flavor and strikes a perfect balance with the sweetness of the vanilla and sugar. Use it to top desserts, berries or anywhere that you might use whipped cream.

Combine and then whip the cream and the Fromage Blanc in a mixing bowl. Shortly before it's stiff, add the sugar and the vanilla. Continue whipping just until the cream will hold a good stiff peak when the beaters are lifted. Spread on the cooled layers. Chill until ready to serve. Will hold nicely for hours in the fridge.

Peanut Butter Mudd Pie with Espresso Caramel Sauce

This dessert has a lot of elements to it but isn't at all difficult. Just be sure to allow plenty of time for freezing the layers in between steps. You will also want to make your sugar syrup for the gelato in advance. This makes a really nice summer birthday cake and has the added bonus of wanting to be made in advance, letting you get it out of the way the day before!

CRUST

1½ cups chocolate wafer cookie crumbs, like Nabisco chocolate wafers

4 tablespoons butter

2 tablespoons sugar

GELATO

2 cups water

1½ cups brown sugar

1 cup organic Valencia peanut butter, chilled

1 (5 ½-ounce) tub Harley Farms fromage blanc, or 4 ounces fresh chèvre, chilled

12 ounces chocolate fudge, like Hershey or Scharffenberger, warmed

Espresso Carmel Sauce

1 cup honey-roasted peanuts, crushed

CRUST

Process the cookies in the food processor, or crush the cookies by putting them in a ziplock and "hammering" them with a rolling pin or something heavy and unbreakable. Melt the butter in a medium saucepan; add the cookie crumbs and sugar, and combine. Press the mixture into a 9- or 10-inch springform. Wrap in plastic and freeze.

GELATO

Combine the water and brown sugar in a small saucepan and bring to a full boil. Remove from heat and chill for several hours or overnight. In the blender, combine the sugar syrup, peanut butter and fromage blanc until smooth. Remove the ice cream bowl from the freezer, set in place and make the gelato according to the machine's instructions. When the gelato is ready, spoon it onto the frozen chocolate crust, smoothing out the surface. Cover and return the pan to the freezer right away. Freeze for at least 2 hours.

When the gelato has set in the freezer, spoon the warm chocolate fudge over it, smooth it out, cover and freeze until firm.

To serve, remove from the freezer. Let sit 10 minutes. Remove the springform's ring. Slice with a large sharp knife. Serve with a little of the Espresso Caramel Sauce and a sprinkle of the crushed peanuts.

Espresso Caramel Sauce

You can make this sauce a day or two in advance, if need be.

½ cup freshly brewed espresso (2 shots)

½ cup sugar

½ cup Meyenberg Evaporated Goat Milk or cream

3 tablespoons unsalted butter

Pinch salt

In a heavy saucepan, combine the coffee and sugar. Bring to a boil and reduce the liquid by half. Whisk in the evaporated milk. Bring to a full boil for 1 minute. Remove from heat. When cooled down, add the butter and salt, whisking until smooth. Pour into a small pitcher or glass measuring cup and cover with plastic wrap. Refrigerate for at least an hour.

Bananny Cake with Cream Cheese Icing

1	cup mashed ripe bananas
2	bananas, sliced
½	cup brown sugar
½	cup real maple syrup, plus a little extra for brushing on layers
2	extra-large free-range eggs
½	cup canola oil
½	cup whole milk yogurt (goat yogurt if you have it!)
½	teaspoon vanilla
1¾	cups all-purpose flour
1	teaspoon baking soda
½	teaspoon baking powder
½	teaspoon salt
¾	cup crushed walnuts (optional)

CREAM CHEESE ICING

3	cups powdered sugar
4	tablespoons unsalted butter, softened
4	ounces fromage blanc or chèvre
½	teaspoon vanilla

I made this cake for a family gathering one spring, and the next morning my sister-in-law called. "I have an emergency," she explained. "Oh, no, is little Sammy sick?" I asked. "Not exactly, but we're out of the banana cake leftovers you sent home! I need that recipe!" Kids really love this.

Preheat oven to 350 degrees F. Butter or oil two 9-inch-round cake pans. Mash the banana in a large bowl. Beat in the brown sugar and maple syrup until smooth. Add the eggs, one at a time. Then stir in the oil, yogurt and vanilla.

Combine the dry ingredients and add half to the banana mixture. Beat until just mixed. Add the remainder of the dry ingredients and combine. Pour into prepared cake pans and bake for about 25–30 minutes. You will know when the cake is close to being done because the aroma will tell you! Remove from the oven when the cake is golden brown and the top is springy. After 10 minutes, turn out onto a wire cooling rack. Wait to frost until it is completely cool.

CREAM CHEESE ICING
Place the frosting ingredients in a bowl and combine with an electric mixer until very smooth. To assemble the cake, brush a little maple syrup on the first layer and cover with the sliced bananas. Top with the second layer. Spread the icing on the top and sides.

Bartlett Pear Tart with Honey and Fromage Blanc

CRUST

1¼ cups all-purpose or whole-wheat pastry flour, plus a little more for rolling

1 tablespoons sugar

¼ teaspoon salt

6 tablespoons very cold unsalted butter

1 egg yolk

2 tablespoons ice cold water

PEAR FILLING

4–5 large ripe Bartlett pears, peeled, if you like, and sliced

1 teaspoon cinnamon

¼ teaspoon cloves

2 tablespoons sugar

2 tablespoons all-purpose flour

2 tablespoons butter

¼ cup honey

3 ounces fromage blanc

1 egg white

There is nothing quite like the taste of a perfectly ripe Bartlett pear. Pick them or buy them just a tiny bit green and let them ripen inside a brown paper bag for a day or two in a cool spot. When you open the bag and get a whiff of their perfume you'll know it's time for the tart! Try this with Red Bartletts instead, if you can get them, and leave the skins on—they are beautiful!

CRUST

Combine the flour, sugar and salt in a mixing bowl or in the bowl of a food processor. Slice the butter, add to the flour mixture and work with a pastry blender, or pulse in the processor, until the mixture is the texture of coarse cornmeal. In a small bowl, combine the yolk and water. Add it to the flour and butter mixture tossing it with a fork or gently pulse the machine until the dough begins to come together into a ball.

Turn the dough out onto a board sprinkled with a little more flour. Give the dough a few kneads and press into a flattened round. At this point, you can chill or store the dough, but I like to roll it out right away and get it into the tart pan. Flour a rolling pin and roll the dough into a 12-inch circle. Transfer the dough to a 9-inch tart pan and press into place, folding the raw edges back a little so that they look nice. Let the smoothed edge extend a little beyond the rim of the pan, as it will shrink slightly during baking. Slip the whole thing into the freezer for about 15 minutes while you Preheat oven to 400 degrees F (or cover and freeze until ready to use) and prepare the fruit.

PEAR FILLING

Toss the pears gently with the cinnamon, cloves, sugar and flour. Set aside. Melt the butter and honey in a medium bowl in the microwave. Whisk in the fromage blanc and stir until smooth. Add the pear mixture, tossing gently to coat.

Once the oven is hot, brush the bottom of the crust with a little egg white and prebake for 10 minutes. Remove from the oven and fill with the pears. Turn the oven down to 375 degrees F and bake on a baking sheet for about 35–40 minutes. A sprinkle of cinnamon sugar puts a finishing touch on the tart. Eat the tart at room temperature for the best flavor.

Chèvre, the baby darling of goat cheese, spends its first night warming in the pasteurizer, its second draining in the cheesecloth and its third as the special guest at dinner.

A Beginner's Guide to Goat Cheese

There are so many different kinds of goat cheese the world over that a person could devote an entire career to studying them and still never taste them all. I can't even begin to cover them here on just a few pages except to provide a visual guide and quick overview to help you choose the right style of cheese for serving and for cooking these recipes.

As a relatively recent convert to goat cheeses, I am amazed at the variety of choices in the local grocery stores these days. In just the last few years, the numbers of new goat cheeses at the cheese counters have soared! Everything from soft fresh chèvre, soft-ripened-style cheeses like Brie, semi-soft cheeses like jack, cheddar and assorted Goudas to hard cheeses, grating cheeses and blues. There are goat cheeses in almost every style you can think of.

Ignorance can be bliss at the cheese counter, if you ask me. Find yourself a good cheese shop or cheese department and ask for help finding something new that appeals to you. The cheese seller's job is to help you select the right cheese and to offer you tastes of the cheeses. Every store has its own hand-picked selection made up of imported and domestic cheeses, and usually the latest in local offerings, all chosen by their own cheese buyer. As well as helping you select the right cheeses, your cheese seller can give you hints on how much to buy and how to store and serve the cheeses, even recommending an appropriate complementary wine. It helps to tell the cheese person what you are planning to do with the cheese: a small assortment of goat cheeses for an appetizer board, a nice melting cheese for a panini, something to put in an omelette or on a pizza, a cheese to make a fondue, etc. Use the suggestions on the following pages as a starting point to help you zero in on what to ask for when you are looking at a huge sea of choices in the cheese shop. Try something new—a little knowledge can be so delicious!

Harley Farms Chive and Dill logs rest on a full wheel of Fraga Mozzarella and a block of Fraga Farmhouse. Bottom left are Harley Farm's flowered Van Goat and a small round of French truffled chévre. Wrapped in leaves are two of Capriale's O'Bahon. A patterned round of Harley Farm ricotta sits behind Cypress Grove's Purple Haze. The tiny Harley Farms Monet and two small scoops of their fromage sit out in front on the right.

Soft Fresh Goat Cheese

This familiar category of goat cheese is made from pasteurized milk and is aged only a few days to a few weeks, depending on the particular style. The most familiar of these is *chèvre*. Barely a couple of days old, chèvre is typically mild and creamy, and has that lovely subtle tang. Fresh chèvre is sold plain, rolled in herbs, or garnished with dried fruits, nuts, flowers, lavender blossoms, etc. Use plain or herbed anywhere you'd use cream cheese—spread on sandwiches, wraps and bagels, crumbled on soups and salads, and added to pasta dishes. Use the flavored varieties on a baguette or on your morning toast.

Fromage blanc and *ricotta* are also just a few days old and are incredibly versatile for use in desserts, lasagne and omelettes, as well as eaten just as is.

Goat *mozzarella* is made with whole goat's milk and is just two days old when it's ready for sale. Perfect on pizza and in lasagne and paninis.

Other styles of fresh goat cheese may be as much as a few weeks old. *Feta* falls roughly into this category but has a more intense flavor than its soft fresh cousins, providing the perfect finishing touch on soups, salads, pizzas and gratins.

Redwood Hill's Camellia, Bucheret and Crottin, and Vermont Butter and Cheese Company's tiny Bijou sit atop a full wheel of Florette French goat Brie. To the right of them, Cypress Grove's Mad River roll sits atop a wedge of their Humboldt Fog. In the center is Monte Enebro from Spain, with Cypress Grove's Truffle Tremor and Bermuda Triangle in front. On the far right in the back is Queso Leonara from Spain, and the logs in front of it are Juniper Grove's Bûche with the wheat sprig and St. Maura ashed from the Loire Valley.

Soft-Ripened Goat Cheese

This category of cheese is hugely popular, especially for picnics and hors d'oeuvres. We love our brie and camembert and must smear millions of pounds of it annually on our French bread. *Brie* and *camembert*-style cheeses made from goat's milk are every bit as interesting as their bovine counterparts and are widely available in many shapes and sizes. You'll find rounds large and small, discs, logs sliced or whole, triangles, pyramids and even squares. Many of the cut wedges of goat brie you'll see for sale will be French, but small whole brie cheeses are popular with American producers. Soft-ripened rounds sometimes called *crottins* or logs sometimes called *buches* from France's Loire Valley are plentiful, but American goat cheese makers are quickly catching up and providing us with our own versions of these styles that previously were imported only from France. Look for goat cheeses made in California by Redwood Hill Goat Dairy in Sebastopol, the organic Elk Creamery in Mendocino, Pug's Leap Petit Marceau from Healdsburg, Rouge et Noir Cheeses from Marin County and Cypress Grove Cheese in Arcata, who makes the wildly popular Humboldt Fog. Other favorites include Vermont Butter & Cheese Company's tiny crottin called Bijou, Juniper Grove's Buche from Oregon and Salt Spring Island Creamery's Juliet and Blue Juliet from the Gulf Islands of Canada.

Clockwise, twelve o'clock: Juniper Grove's Tumalo Tomme from Oregon, which is semifirm in texture but is bathed often while it ages; a wedge of Clisson from France; Brunet, which actually should be pictured with the soft-ripened group, practically melts for you at room temperature; and three precious little Bocconcino di Pura Capra from Italy.

Washed-Rind Goat Cheese

This is an intensely flavored category of cheeses. Some members of this category might even be considered downright stinky, but the smell can be more overwhelming than the taste. Washed-rind cheeses are just that—bathed in liquids as they age so that the rinds stay soft and supple. Though typically soft and creamy, cheeses in this category can range from very soft and even gooey all the way to semifirm. Tastes can range from somewhat mild to very, very assertive.

Until recently, many of the cheeses in this category found at the cheese counter were imported largely from France, like Clisson, a nice mild semisoft cheese whose rind is washed in Sauterne. An Italian gem of a washed rind is the little Bocconcini di Pura Capra—a small, creamy round with a very approachable flavor. New washed rind cheeses are appearing on the scene from United States cheese artisans. Look for Juniper Grove's Tumalo Tomme, Cabra La Mancha, a manchego style from Firefly Farms in Maryland, River's Edge Illahee Tomme, rubbed in truffle oil, and their Saint Olga, which is washed in local beer! Haystack Mountain in Colorado makes Sunlight and Red Cloud. The popular Mont Saint Francis from Capriole Dairy in Indiana has the distinction of being one of the first washed-rind cheeses made in the United States.

Clockwise, one o'clock: A wedge of Arina Goat Gouda stands on end. Clisson sits atop a slice of Rumiano Goat Cheddar, Queso de Cabra with its reddish rind, a quarter round of Sally Jackson Goat, Meyenberg Chive and Garlic Jack, a wedge of Drunken Goat on an uncut round and a square of caramel-colored Norwegian Gjetost. In the center sits a wedge of Tomme de la Châtaigneraie.

Semisoft **Goat Cheese**

This familiar category contains the young jack, gouda and cheddar-style cheeses we use for so many things. The milk from which they are made can be raw or pasteurized; cheeses aged over sixty days are allowed to be made from unpasteurized milk. Semisoft cheeses are typically aged for three to six months. They will usually be mild, smooth and creamy but firm enough to slice. Cheeses in this category are suitable for countless uses in everyday cooking. Think paninis, enchiladas, pizzas, quesadillas, burgers, sandwiches—just about anything you may want to put cheese on. The cheese counters are overflowing with semisoft goat from France, like Clisson and Tomme de la Chataignerai, and young goudas from Holland. Spanish cheeses are abundant as well, like Murcia al Vino (the drunken goat), with its beautiful wine-soaked purple rind and newcomer Cabra Romero, with its rosemary-crusted rind. From domestic producers there is cheddar from Cypress Grove and a tasty raw milk goat cheddar by Rumiano in northern California. Goat jack from Greenbanks Farms and Sally Jackson Goat from Washington State are unique semisofts. Carr Valley in Wisconsin makes the wonderful Cocoa Cardona with its coating of cocoa powder!

Clockwise, twelve o-clock: Fenacho Gouda from Tumalo Farms, a half round of Twig Farm Goat, Midnight Moon, aged goat Gouda from Cypress Grove, Garrotxa with the Montcabrer just behind it, Montebon mixed milk cheese in left front, Juniper Grove's Tumalo Tomme behind it and Love Tree Farm's Old Goat Tomme in the black rind on the far left.

Semifirm **Goat Cheese**

As the name implies, this group is firmer in texture than the semisoft category. More liquid is pressed out in the cheese-making process, and the cheese is aged longer, resulting in a firmer and deeper-flavored, lower-moisture cheese. This firm style will keep much longer than the less-aged semisoft cheese. Cheeses from this category include *aged cheddar, aged jack, aged gouda, manchego* styles and others. Le Chèvre Noir from Canada makes wonderful aged goat cheddar wrapped in black wax. Aged goudas are readily available as well. Try Midnight Moon from Cypress Grove to set off your cheese board or grate some in frittatas and pastas. There are Spanish manchego styles like Ibores and Murcia Curado, or Naked Goat with that characteristic dry flakey texture when sliced. These Spanish manchego styles pair well with green olives and herbs in appetizers and frittatas, and are perfect for melting on rustic bread or in quesadillas. For a cheese fondue, try Hillman's Harvest from New York State, Capricious from Achadinha Cheese Company in Petaluma or the wonderful Tumalo Tomme from Juniper Grove that sits on the fence between semisoft and semifirm. Lovetree Farm Old Goat Tomme from Wisconsin is firm but smooth and has a wonderful color and a hint of caramel. All of these are wonderful and have endless possibilities in cooking.

Capra Pimentao is on the left, with its beautiful paprika-coated rind. Capra Sarda from Sardinia sits atop Cabralinda by Nicalau Farms in Modesto and a half wheel of Bodega Shepard from Lakeport.

Hard Goat Cheese

This category takes semifirm one step further. These cheeses are typically aged from six months to a year and sometimes longer. Think *Parmesan* and *Romano* style! While these are the perfect grating cheeses, they are also a super intensely flavored group perfect for the finish on a cheese board.

Salty by nature, these are the perfect cheeses to shave on your fresh salad, dust over your pasta creations or put on a bruschetta as a finishing touch. Spanish Majorero from the Canary Islands falls into this category. It is said that tapas originated with the tradition of serving a slice of this style of cheese sitting atop a glass of sherry. Capra Sarda, also from Sardinia, grates beautifully and works really well for dishes like the Saffron Fettuccine Carbonara (page 98). Capra Pimentao, from Spain, is delicious on a cheese board as well as in cooking. The new Cabralinda from Nicalau Farms in Modesto, California, is one of the rare domestic cheeses that falls into this well-aged category, as is the shepherd's cheese from Yerba Santa Dairy in Lakeport that takes it flavors from the wild herbs the goats browse on.

Clockwise, twelve o'clock: A wedge of Carr Valley Billy Blue rests atop its French cousin Blue du Bocage. A slice of Valdeón, a mixed milk blue, is on the right wrapped in a neat covering of leaves. Herve Mons Persille Chèvre du Beaujolais is out front, and a wedge of Legendairy Blue Gouda stands on end to the left.

Goat **Blues**

Lovers of *blue cheese* may be surprised to know that there are so many choices of goat blue to be found. Besides the typical mottled blue-veined cheeses we are used to seeing, there are soft-ripened blues of different sorts, where the blue is primarily on the outside, as well as aged caramel-colored blues with extremely intense flavors. Many are from Europe, France in particular. Pascal Beillevaire's Blue du Bocage is a well-known French favorite, as is the very well-aged raw milk Herve Mons Persille Chèvre du Beaujolais. From Holland, there is Legendairy's Blue Gouda, a well-aged caramel-colored goat blue. Salt Spring Island Creamery makes Blue Juliet, a soft-ripened blue cheese that's worth a trip to the islands for!

United States artisan cheese makers are beginning to produce some great goat blues. Carr Valley Cheese in Wisconsin makes the lovely mild Billy Blue, perfect for crumbling on salads. Rouge et Noir from California makes a camembert-style blue called Marin Chèvre Blue. Westfield Farms in Massachusetts makes several goat blues, including their Classic Blue Log. Firefly Farms in Maryland makes Mountain Top Blue. Lively Run Goat Dairy in New York State is one of the oldest goat dairies in the United States, established 1982, and makes the popular Cayuga Blue.

Clockwise, two o'clock: A wedge of Blue Valdeón, made from a mixture of goat's and cow's milk, a small wedge taken from the French soft-ripened three-milk round La Tur beside it, a piece of Greek Halloumi-style cheese made from sheep and goat's milk, and in the upper left-hand corner the Montebon, made from all three milks.

Mixed Milk **Cheese**

Many cheese makers make mixed milk cheeses either to fine-tune the flavor or perhaps the texture or to use what they have on hand. For whatever reason, some wonderful mixed milk cheeses are available. Aside from the imported mixed milk selections pictured above, there are lots of domestic dairies making differing styles of cheeses with mixed milk. Andante Dairy in Petaluma makes a couple of soft mixed milk cheeses called Figaro and Minuet. Paula Lambert's Mozzerella Company in Texas makes a mozzarella called Capriella, which is a blend of goat and cow's milk.

One that I have recently discovered is Carr Valley's Mobay, which is two layers, one of sheep and one of goat, separated by a thin layer of ash. The pale yellow of the sheep's milk layer is a subtle contrast to the very white layer of the goat's. I like to set a wedge of this one next to a wedge of Humboldt Fog, a soft ripened goat's cheese to mimic the look of the ash running through the middle. The two cheeses are very different, but it's fun to create cheese boards that are not only pleasing to the palate but also to the eye.

On the **Cheese Trail**

I could have listed a hundred-plus goat dairies here, as there is surely one near you; but, instead, I have listed some Web sites that keep fairly up-to-date information on the hundreds of artisan cheeses and dairies around the country. As I began my work on this resource section, I figured I'd find several dozen goat farms to investigate for my book. My list kept getting longer and longer, and soon it was reaching a hundred entries. I wondered how to narrow it down and still have a great list of resources. Every search turned up new cheese makers, new goat farms, new Web sites and news articles about goat cheese from all over the United States. And then one day, Amazon.com, from whom I'd just bought a few cheese books, sent me an e-mail. Jeffrey Roberts had just published a book called *The Atlas of American Artisan Cheese*! Not only was that an amazing coincidence, it was a welcome one! I quickly got hold of a copy. This fabulous resource references 345 artisan cheese makers in the United States. Not only was my task done, but everything I needed to know was right in front of me. There are about two hundred entries in the goat farm index alone! That is possibly ten times the number of goat farms there were about twenty years ago. I highly recommend getting a copy of this book and taking a look for yourself at all the new cheese makers in your part of the country. So, I have streamlined this source section to be practical. I have listed just a few favorite goat dairies but have included some Web sites that can direct you to all the cheese events and cheese makers near you.

Web sites:

American Cheese Society
www.cheesesociety.org

California Artisan Cheese Guild
www.cacheeseguild.org

Cheese-related articles by Janet Fletcher
www.sfgate.com

Fork and Bottle
www.forkandbottle.com

New England Cheesemaking Supply Company
www.cheesemaking.com

Pacific Northwest Cheese Project
www.pnwcheese.typepad.com

Sonoma Cheese Festival (annual event)
www.artisancheesefestival.com

Great Places to Buy a Wide Variety of Goat Cheeses

24th Street Cheese Company
3893-24th Street, San Francisco, CA
(415) 821-6658

The Cheeseboard
1504 Shattuck Ave., Berkeley, CA
www.cheeseboardcollective.coop

Cowgirl Creamery
(in San Francisco's Ferry Plaza, Point
Reyes Station and Washington, D.C.)
www.cowgirlcreamery.com

Draeger's Markets
(Menlo Park, Los Altos, San Mateo and
Blackhawk)
www.draegers.com

Half Moon Bay Wine & Cheese
604 Main Street, Half Moon Bay, CA
(650) 726-1520
www.hmbwineandcheese.com

Robert's Market (since 1889)
3015 Woodside Road, Woodside, CA
www.robertsmarket.com

Say Cheese
856 Cole Street. San Francisco, CA
(415) 665-5020

Sigona's Farmers Market
Redwood City, CA, and Stanford Shopping Center, Palo Alto, CA
www.sigonas.com

Whole Foods Markets
(270 stores in North America and the
United Kingdom—that is a lot of cheese!)
www.wholefoodsmarket.com

Some of My Favorite Producers of Artisan Goat Cheese

Achadinha Cheese Company (since 2004)
owner/cheese maker Donna Pacheco,
Pacheco Dairy, Petaluma, CA
Farmstead cheeses—Capricious (aged)
and Broncha (a ricotta-salata style)

San Francisco's Ferry Plaza Farmer's
Market and San Raphael's Marin
Farmer's Market
www.achadinha.com

Capriole Goat Cheese
owner/cheese maker Judy Schad
Greenville, IN
Farmstead goat cheeses—O'Banon
wrapped in Kentucky bourbon-soaked

chestnut leaves, Wabash cannonball.
www.capriolegoatcheese.com

Carr Valley Cheese Company
owner/cheese maker Sid Cook
La Valle, WI
Farmstead goat, sheep and cow
cheeses—Billy Blue, Cocoa Cardona,
Mobay.
www.carrvalleycheese.com

Cypress Grove
owner/cheese maker Mary Keehn
Arcata, CA
Farmstead goat cheeses—Mad River
Roll, Humboldt Fog, Bermuda Triangle,
Purple Haze, Midnight Moon and more.
www.cypressgrovechevre.com

Elk Creamery
Mendocino County, CA, (707) 877-1719
Organic farmstead goat cheeses—Black
Gold, Red Gold, Camembert.
www.elkcreamery.com

Drake Family Farms
owners/cheese makers Jeanette and
Ron Drake
West Jordan, UT, (801) 255-MILK
www.drakefamilyfarms.com

Fraga Farm
owners/cheese makers Janice and
Larry Neilson
Sweet Home, OR, (541) 367-3891
Organic farmstead goat cheeses—
chèvre, Goatzarella, aged feta, farmhouse wheel, aged Cheddar.
www.fragafarm.com

Harley Farms Goat Dairy
owner/cheese maker Dee Harley
205 North Street, Pescadero, CA
(650) 879-0480
Dairy shop open daily. Call for a
Saturday tour.
Farmstead goat cheeses—chèvre, feta,
ricotta, fromage blanc.
www.harleyfarms.com

Juniper Grove
owner E. Pierre Kolisch
Redmond, OR, (541) 923-8353
Farmstead goat cheeses—Tumalo Tomme.
www.junipergrovefarm.com

Pug's Leap Farm
owners Pascal Destandan and Eric Smith
Healdsburg, CA, (707) 433-1021
Farmstead goat cheeses—Bûche, Pave,
Petit Marceau.
www.pugsleap.com

Redwood Hill Farms
owner/cheese maker Jennifer Bice
Sebastapol, CA, (707) 823-8250
Farmstead goat cheeses—goat yogurt,
chèvre, feta, Cheddar and soft-ripened
cheeses like Camellia, Bucheret,
California Crottin.
www.redwoodhill.com

Salt Spring Island Creamery
owners David and Nancy Wood
Salt Spring Island, BC, Canada,
(250) 653-2300
Artisan goat cheeses

Bodega & Yerba Santa Goat Dairy
owners/cheese makers Javier and
Daniel Salmon

Lakeport, CA, (707) 263-8131
Farmstead goat cheeses—chèvre,
Chevito, Shepherd's cheese and tubs of
Peruvian goat caramel called Bodega
Natilla.

Great Books on Cheese

Eyewitness French Cheeses. DK Publish-
ing: London. 2005.

Fletcher, Janet. *The Cheese Course.*
Chronicle Books: SF. 2000.

———. *Cheese & Wine: A Guide to Se-
lecting, Pairing and Enjoying.* Chronicle
Books: SF. 2007.

McCalman, Max and David Gibbons.
Cheese. Potter: NY. 2005.

Murray's Cheese Handbook. Broadway
Books: NY. 2006.

Roberts, Jeffrey. *The Atlas of American
Artisan Cheese.* Chelsea Green Publish-
ing: VT. 2007.

Werlin, Laura. *The All American Cheese
and Wine Book.* Stewart, Tabori & Chang:
NY. 2003.

———. *Cheese Essentials.* Stewart, Tabori
& Chang: NY. 2007.

Goat Research

University of Granada, "Goats' Milk
Is More Beneficial Than Cows' Milk,
Study Suggests." *Science Daily.* (July 31,
2007). http://www.sciencedaily.com/
releases/2007/07/070730100229.htm
(accessed January 14, 2008).

Other Favorite Sources

Art Culinaire (LaCanche ranges and
Woodinville Wines)
www.frenchranges.com and
www.woodinvillewines.com

Epiphany Gourmet
www.epiphanygourmet.com

Meyenberg Goat Milk Products
www.meyenberg.com

Index

Metric Conversion Chart

Liquid and Dry Measures

U.S.	Canadian	Australian
¼ teaspoon	1 mL	1 ml
½ teaspoon	2 mL	2 ml
1 teaspoon	5 mL	5 ml
1 tablespoon	15 mL	20 ml
¼ cup	50 mL	60 ml
⅓ cup	75 mL	80 ml
½ cup	125 mL	125 ml
⅔ cup	150 mL	170 ml
¾ cup	175 mL	190 ml
1 cup	250 mL	250 ml
1 quart	1 liter	1 litre

Temperature Conversion Chart

Fahrenheit	Celsius
250	120
275	140
300	150
325	160
350	180
375	190
400	200
425	220
450	230
475	240
500	260

chèvre

soft fresh goat cheese

ricotta

fromage blanc

car

crottins

brie logs

soft-ripened goat cheese

gouda

wash-rind goat cheese

cheddar

jack

gouda